Tommy Transit's Bus Tales:

How to Change the World from 9 to 5

Or as a Bus Driver, 7 to 9am and back for the evening rush hour
(but my editor says that's too long a title!)

By Tom Tompkins and Michele Hall

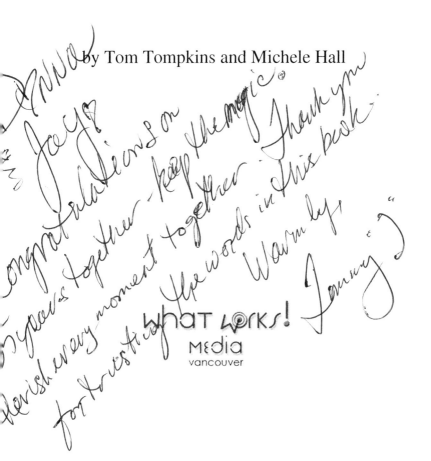

what works!
MEDIA
vancouver

*This book is dedicated to my fellow bus drivers,
as well as the thousands of passengers who
boarded my bus for the past twenty years,
bringing stories, fun and inspiration.*

Cover design and layout by Michele Hall
Photography by Olivia Fermi
Editing by Sue Chambers

Copyright © 2012 by Tom Tompkins
and Michele Hall
www.TommyTransit.com

Published in Canada by
What Works Media, Vancouver, BC
www.WhatWorksMedia.ca

ISBN: 978-0-9880002-1-6
Printed in Canada
First Edition

Contents

Tom's Foreword

I never thought I'd grow up to be one of these: a transit operator. Even though it's a job many people feel is low on the social scale, I take great pride in who I am and what I do. I get people to and from their office, school or doctor appointments safely. I believe that public transit is an essential service that cuts down on the number of cars on the road and the amount of pollution that goes into the environment. And most importantly, I have been able to turn a so-called 'simple' job into one that makes a difference to my own well-being and job satisfaction by discovering a way to contribute positively to the lives of hundreds of thousands of people. In short, my job is very fulfilling.

My grandmother had grander visions for me. She wanted me to be an architect. It was a good profession, paid well and was prestigious at a time when social standing was everything. She thought little of her husband's position as a rose gardener and only slightly better of my father's job as a sewing machine sales and repairman. I never followed the career that granny saw for me, but like so many of us who came of age in the sixties, I explored life by doing a wide range of jobs from swabbing decks on oil rigs in the Arctic to playing washboard in a professional Barbershop Blues band, installing telephone lines and running my own photography company at Expo '86 in Vancouver. Did I also mention I sold frozen steak and seafood door to door? Phew! Quite a range!

My mother also believed in me and told me constantly that I could be anything that I put my mind to. Her faith in my abilities was the strongest kind of love a child can receive and it carried me fearlessly through my childhood and beyond. While school was not my forte, to say the least, I did excel in sports and made my mark by running the 100-yard dash in eleven seconds flat—very close to Olympic standards at the time.

When I won a public speaking contest at age twelve, it was my mother who helped me overcome stage fright by suggesting that I picture the students sitting naked in their seats. Perhaps she had read it somewhere and suggested it to me as a last resort to build my confidence as the day drew closer, but it worked like a charm to push away my nervousness, keep my sense of humour, delight my (naked) audience and win the competition. Thanks Mom!

The older I get, the more I see my father's loving influence in everything I do. With his quirky and sometimes embarrassing sense of humour that I only truly appreciated much later in life, my Dad demonstrated his inherent desire to connect with others and share his joy of life. What once was a source of personal discomfort, I now see as his kind and generous way of always being of service to others.

I clearly recall the day I was sitting on a bench with my Dad waiting for a bus in the small town of Whitby where I grew up. All of a sudden he jumped up and dashed off. I was confused, wondering where he had gone. Then I caught sight of him opening a door for a woman carrying a load of groceries to her car. He even risked us missing our bus by holding her bags so she could load them into the trunk the way she wanted. "Who is that lady?" I asked when he came back. "I don't know," he replied.

Puzzled, I asked, "Why did you run over to help her? We might have missed our bus." He turned and smiled at me, "Son, it's simply the right thing to do." Acts like that had an enormous impact on who I am today. Thanks Dad!

To Michele

This section may be the only collection of words that do not pass through the magic magnifying glass and filter of wise discernment of my amazing co-writer Michele Hall. As she reminds me, she is the writer and I am the "co". There would be no book without her.

Words fail me in an attempt to describe the value of her contribution to this book and to my life. I had all the ideas and the thoughts for some years now, but the book's gestation period eventually had a deadline and the pressure was on. After twenty years with transit I was tired of schedules and deadlines, so this was a task of immense proportions for me. Michele guided me from one step to the other during this whole incredible process. When I started, I had no idea of all the work to be done in writing a book. I look at books very differently now. I see all that goes into creating one: the front and back cover, the acknowledgements, the endorsements, the table of contents, editing, formatting, printing, choosing fonts, advertising the launch, publicity, selfless promotion and overseeing the larger plan.

Considering my tendency to be a bit ADHD, Michele had her work cut out for her long before the book became real for me. After the last few months I think she could qualify as a coach, mentor, mother, sister, medical advisor, counsellor, confidante and whip-mistress. Many hats were worn by my best friend of the past nine years, and all were fashion statements! Her qualifications are varied: TV Producer/Director, published author, ghost-writer, book coach, graphic designer, marketing specialist, producer of magical ideas and the list goes on. I hope the outpouring of my love and kinship will give her just an inkling of the impact she has had on my heart and soul. A simple thank you is far too short to remotely express the gratitude I feel for all she has done and continues to do.

I offered to take her out for dinner on the town. In typical Michele fashion, she chose Athens. Reservations to a charming restaurant overlooking the Aegean Sea will be made. To Michele I will be indebted for life as she enriches me in a myriad of ways. Namaste, Michele I am deeply, heartfully yours.

To My Fellow Drivers

I'd like to acknowledge all my co-workers for their tolerance and patience with my antics over the years as I spiralled into realms of silliness in the enjoyment of my job. I appreciate their encouragement and enjoyment of me in my eagerness to serve along with my wacky sense of humor for the purpose of making anyone laugh that was able. No one came within ten feet of me without some fun jumping into their pockets.

Coast Mountain Bus Company, Vancouver, B.C. needs to be honored for the support they offer all the drivers. I personally want to thank all the supervisors, trainers, depot clerks, management and cafeteria staff who assisted me during my twenty-year journey. I felt totally supported and nurtured by all the programs and services available to us.

My dear friend Jon Scott was the most consistent prodder in gently nudging me to finish writing the book I had started so long ago. Each time I saw him he would be friendly and sociable and yet always managed to drop into the conversation, as though it were an afterthought, "Hey Tommy, how is that Bus Tales book of yours coming along?" His persistent reminders acted on my conscience like a true friend who makes sure you are going to climb your own personal Mount Everest, come Hell or high water. Then to seal his support for me, he purchased two copies of the completed book. Thanks Jon, you rock.

Thank you collectively to the CTV news crew that hung out with me on my bus for over an hour on my 60th birthday and to the Vancouver Province newspaper for the feature article on me that appeared a few weeks later. Together you helped me overcome any niggling doubts I may have had that I had good cause to put my thoughts on paper.

I also wish to give a great big thanks to my passengers who have daily inspired me over the past twenty years. Many of you were willing to play and have fun with me either in verbal exchanges, witty jokes or interesting anecdotes. It was you who provided the motivation to write this book in the first place. I couldn't have done it without you and your inspiration. You are wonderful.

Tom Tompkins, aka Tommy Transit
Vancouver, Canada

Michele's Foreword

From the first moment I met Tom, I knew he was what you could call an 'extraordinary' ordinary person. Although he didn't have an impressive career or a long list of credentials following his name, he had one thing that makes him stand out from most people: he is a happy man. This is even more remarkable as I met Tom at what was possibly the darkest time in his life. His second marriage had collapsed, he was going through a personal bankruptcy and his beloved dog had just died. The place he chose to live as newly single man happened to be the shared home I lived in with my brother, my nine-year-old daughter and three other roommates. Tom's effervescence and cheerful nature was an immediate draw, and he brought life and fun to the house.

Over the years, Tom has impressed me with his unbounded enthusiasm for life and for the joy he gets from connecting with people. I can honestly say I have never met anyone more out-going. He is constantly calling friends and organizing get togethers. Even before our relationship became personal and romantic, he would come home from work filled with delightful tales of his interactions with people on the bus. Almost every one began with, "So, I met this guy on the bus and..." As a long-time storyteller, I eventually said, "Tom, you need to write a book." Years and many, many revisions and rewrites later, we now have a book that only gives the reader the tiniest glimpse of how out-going, happy to serve, and big-hearted Tom is in person.

Again and again, as we went over the wording of the book, he would ask me, "Am I being arrogant in saying this?" And I would assure him that he had a very important message to share. People everywhere feel stuck in jobs and relationships that don't bring them happiness or satisfaction. Tom has a truly unique and playful way of interacting with others that makes people feel good about themselves. Like a child's laughter, Tom's message is infectious and invites us all to join in.

I, perhaps more than anyone, was aware of the potential for his extraordinarily simple message to make a huge impact on others, especially those who work with the public. Over the years I have put into practice many of the ways he interacts with others – to wonderful effect. I was fascinated when I started studying Vedic wisdom and learned that Tom's Art of Acknowledgement is one of the 64 Vedic Arts – the art of the compliment.

I am honoured to support Tom in the many ways I can by getting this book with its easy-to-practice tools and heart-warming stories into your hands.

Michele Hall,
Vancouver

 # Introduction

(For those who don't read intros - read this anyway)

"Don't frown because you never know who's
falling in love with your smile."
~ Xandra Moss, age 13

T he bus door opens.

A queue of people troop onto the bus. Many look bedraggled and tired at the end of their workday. Some struggle with strollers, their little ones cranky after being picked up from daycare. An old man shuffles on the bus and looks around for a place to sit near the front where signs remind passengers that these seats are reserved for the handicapped and elderly. Everyone pretends they don't notice him. A teenage girl stands near the front of the bus yelling loudly to her friend on her cell phone. It would be easy to get pulled into the same mood, to call out loudly, "Move to the back of the bus!"

It would be understandable if I bemoaned the fact that my shift includes the rush hour crush and if I felt impelled to treat everyone the way they treat me – like a mechanical part of the huge sixty-foot articulated city bus I am driving. But that's not my style. And more importantly, it's not my mission.

Although I'd always been outgoing, around the turn of this century I hit a point where I was so depressed that I was on extended stress leave. Both my parents had died within the past few years and my second marriage was falling apart. Financial doom was impending as I went into a personal bankruptcy following the leaky condo disaster that hit many small homeowners in Vancouver. And to top it all off, Pecan, my devoted companion of thirteen years, a German Shorthaired Pointer Lab, died. No matter which way I turned, there was not much joy to be found. All of this occurred within a period of six months. I was sad and tired all the time. Friends and co-workers were shocked that I was still able to walk upright. It was clear to all but me that I needed a change, a big shift.

So what was it that turned things around to the point where only a few years later I was featured in the local newspaper and made the national news on TV for being nothing more than myself? What was it that made me take what most people would call 'a working stiff' type job and turn it into something a lot more than just shuttling people around town? Why was it that people often got on my bus tired and hollow, but soon were laughing and chatting with each other? How was it that what had once seemed an exhausting way of making a living, is now so fun and enjoyable that I am surprised at how an eight or a ten-hour day has just flown by and I am still full of energy?

Well, I discovered a little secret that keeps me motivated, happy, healthy and looking forward to my next day at work. I rarely am home sick and most of the time I'm laughing so hard that at the end of the shift I'm actually hoarse.

My secret? It's a little thing called purpose.

While in the midst of my difficult marriage and unhappy circumstances, I joined the remarkable Brock Tully at his monthly *Porridge for the Soul* breakfast meetings that ran in Vancouver. Brock had cycled across North America promoting his Kindness Foundation and was an inspirational leader in the Vancouver community. To this day, he hosts an annual Kindness Concert, which seems to grow bigger every year. In 2011, it attracted over one thousand people to celebrate and promote the messages of kindness, compassion, love and peace, with the intention of touching the hearts of people around the world. It is so much more than just a concert. It is part of a global movement intended to eliminate violence, bullying, suicide, cruelty and abuse to ourselves, others and the environment. Some of the most inspiring and powerful performing artists come together for a one-of-a-kind concert that focuses on solutions to these issues.

In September 2001, we gathered for our monthly meeting—shocked at the terrorist attacks that had happened a few days earlier in New York City. We wondered if it was futile to try to bring more kindness into a world when thousands of people had just been killed in an outrageously daring act of terror. Our feeble attempts seemed dwarfed by the enormity of a world that appeared to be going crazier than ever. We quickly realized that not only was it NOT futile, but it was imperative for us each to make some kind of positive action that would bit by bit, kind act by kind act, become the solution. Gandhi said it best: "Be the change you want to see in the world."

Almost mechanically we began to share how we could each bring some kindness into our own lives. One entrepreneur mentioned how he could treat his employees with more respect and understanding. A mother spoke about how she had brought a program called "Coin-spiracy" that helps young people see how kind acts can enact positive global change to her children's school. A doctor announced that he wished to be more compassionate with his patients.

I thought about my own job and how easily I could be dismissed because I'm only a bus driver. That's when it hit me. The businessman had a couple of dozen employees, clients and business associates. The mother had her children's school and the doctor had his unending line of patients. But, as I quickly did some calculations, I was astounded. Good grief, I thought. I am in contact with thousands of people every week. In fact, I had the opportunity to be in close proximity—if only for a few seconds—with more than 150,000 people a year. That had to be more than the Queen, the Prime Minister and the Pope rolled together!

I knew that I had in front of me the perfect opportunity to bring a little kindness into other people's lives. Right then and there I made a conscious decision to make a positive, uplifting impression on all my passengers. Little did I realize that it would also dramatically alter my own life. From having to take three months disability leave for stress and depression, today I am known throughout the city as Tommy Transit, bus driver on a mission.

A Tommy T Quip

Hope You Showered!

In the morning rush hour crowd, the bus is packed to the rafters. I glance back to see people swaying from the hanging straps.

I call out over the intercom:
"It is about this time that you may be thinking to yourself, 'I hope everyone had a shower and used deodorant like I did.' Okay, folks. Breathe deep and enjoy the ride."

Chapter 1
What the World Needs Now

"Life is ten percent what happens to you and ninety percent how you respond to it." ~ Lou Holtz

"I used to wait for you," a young woman with long dark hair stood smiling up at me as I waited for my relief bus to arrive. "Didn't you use to drive the B-line?" she added.

"Gee, I haven't driven that for nearly ten years," I reflected.

"Well, I used to make a point to get on your bus because you shared an inspiring quote. You really made my day. I would almost be late for class but your shared thoughts were worth it."

I stood there dumbstruck shaking my head. I had initiated the quote for the day shortly after the discussion about what we could do to make the world a kinder place at the *Porridge for the Soul* meeting. Almost a decade later, she recognized me as the driver who had once brightened her commute. That is one long ripple in the world to last all those years.

Public Inertia

If you've ever ridden public transit, you know that when people clamber aboard a bus they seem turned off, as if the time spent travelling is a kind of numbed out limbo realm that doesn't really count as part of their real life. I had noticed that over the years the situation was actually getting worse as young and old alike got aboard plugged into the latest electronic devices. Technology gives us the illusion that we are more connected, and although we may be connected to those who are far away, we are actually disconnected from all that is going on right in front of us when we are 'plugged in'. In addition to the impassive faces, the atmosphere in the bus is permeated with a dismal, unhappy energy as if it were full of people heading for a day of hard labour at the salt mines rather than what I believe is the truth: that they are participants in the miracle of another precious day in their lives.

If my mission was to make a difference in the lives of hundreds of thousands of people who rode my bus, I was faced with what I could do to bring real fun and joy into people's daily commute and, by extension, into their lives. Was there a way that I could subtly remind them that life also includes small moments of playful interaction? Could I do something that would gently shake up the robotic atmosphere that kept each person isolated in their own protective bubble? You bet I could! It was then and there that I formed a plan of action to gently pull them back to joy.

Putting Joy into Action

Over the years I had amassed quite a collection of quotes that impressed me. Some of these I found in books, some I discovered at personal growth seminars, others I heard at public talks. Perhaps their inspirational wisdom would touch my passengers?

In those days, part of my job was to call out the major streets and bus connections over the loud speaker. With a slight adjustment, I saw my opportunity. I decided to add a thought for the day as I called out the street names. The transfer connections on my bus soon sounded like this:
"I often like to give my passengers a thought for the day in the hope that it helps them on their way: Remember there are a lot more people

27

looking for the right person than working at being the right person. Granville southbound for Richmond, White Rock, the airport and the ferry, north-bound for Downtown. Watch your step please. Thanks for travelling transit. Have a great day."

Eventually the street announcements became automated, and the population of Vancouver became so ethnically diverse that my quote for the day was lost on those who didn't understand English. Although I no longer announced the quote of the day, the young woman reminded me that even a decade later my efforts were not forgotten.

Try A Little Kindness

We all want to belong, to feel special and appreciated. We all want to be seen and feel that we are a part of the greater community. Psychologists have catalogued these feelings into five categories that every human being requires to thrive in life; they are known as Maslow's human hierarchy of needs.

When I look at the chart on the opposite page, I see that self-esteem is an actual ***need***. Yet when I drive around the city, I see that it is in short supply. Instead of self-confident, happy, fulfilled people I see hurt, depression, sadness and pain. It's not my place to know why people are hurting or what is going on in their lives, but I do know that momentarily I am part of their world. It was in this snippet of time where I saw my opportunity to make a difference.

Maslow's Heirarchy of Needs Chart

1. **Biological and Physiological needs** - air, food, drink, shelter, warmth, sex, sleep, etc.
2. **Safety needs** - protection from elements, security, order, law, limits, stability, etc.
3. **Belongingness and Love needs** - work group, family, affection, relationships, etc.
4. **Esteem needs** - self-esteem, achievement, mastery, independence, status, dominance, prestige, managerial responsibility, etc.
5. **Self-Actualization needs** - realizing personal potential, self-fulfillment, seeking personal growth and peak experiences

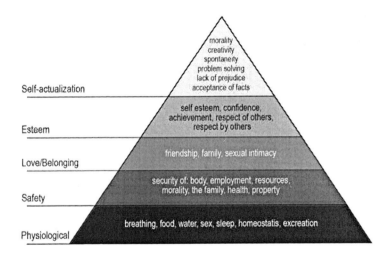

Once I no longer exercised the quote of the day ritual, I wondered what I was going to do to continue my intended mission of reaching out to all the people who travelled on my bus. Was there something else I could undertake that had no language barrier? It was then that I recalled someone by the name of Denis Waitley, whom I had met and befriended years earlier. On several occasions, Denis had come to town and given inspirational talks to a business group I was involved with. His talks were peppered with insights and wisdom. During one speech he said something that remains to this day the single most important statement I have heard in my life:

> *"All we want is to be acknowledged for who we are and the contribution we make. The proof of the truth of this statement is that babies cry for it and grown men die for it." ~ Denis Waitley*

His quote hit me like a bolt of lightning. Could this hunger to be acknowledged be the key to how I would fulfill my mission of bringing more kindness into the world? I already knew I was in the unique position of coming into contact with well over a hundred thousand people a year. I might not have a lot of time – often only seconds – but I now knew what I could do to make a positive difference in the lives of everyone who rode my bus.

A Tommy T Quip

Green Glasses

"Wow very cool glasses, they really suit you."

An older man wearing bright green half frame glasses was inserting his fare into the box.

"Yeah a lot of people tell me that. I don't think they're telling me the truth," he responded.

"Do you know everyone who tells you that?"

"Some, but mostly it's people I've never met that compliment me," he said.

"What if," I suggested, "They were all members of the V.C.G.L.C.?"

"What?" his attention fully captured.

"The 'Vancouver Chapter of the Great Liar's Conspiracy'. During the past few months, you with your very cool bright green glasses have been their target."

I broke into laughter and he heartily joined me in my ability to fabricate magical fun.

"Just say 'thank you' when people compliment you," I said softly to him, "Whether you know them or not, assume they speak from the heart and genuinely like you and your glasses. Have a wonderful day."

"Thanks for the ride...and the fun."

Chapter 2
Changing the Way We Work

"Better to seek change through inspiration than out of desperation." ~ Dennis Waitley

"Y ou're crazy!" people sometimes say when they hear one of my stories. "You're absolutely right." I respond, "It's a prerequisite for my job."

Bus drivers, perhaps more than most others who work with the public, work under very challenging conditions. Every shift, I drive through busy city streets for an average of eight hours with no scheduled meal or bathroom breaks. If I arrive at the end of my route on time, I might get a few minutes downtime before my return trip, but often the circumstances of a growing city slowed down by road construction or aging and handicapped passengers that take longer to board means that I risk running even later simply by going to the washroom. In addition, drivers are often the target of aggression by people feeling alienated by the problems of big city, modern life.

Finally the media has picked up on some of the issues facing bus operators. Dale Carruthers of The London Free Press recently remarked that, *"…when most people think of dangerous jobs, police officer or firefighter comes to mind. But should bus driver be added to the list? Assault, verbal abuse, spitting and even death threats are among the challenges drivers deal with regularly."*

And a study published in the *Journal of Applied Psychology* states that: *"The job of operating public transit vehicles in urban centers may be among the most stressful and unhealthy of modern occupations."*

A sign greets passengers when they board buses in Toronto that says, "Every day at least one TTC worker is assaulted. That's one too many."

How do signs like this fix the problem? Certainly they make us aware of the issue, but is barricading people into plexiglass cages or surrounding them with surveillance cameras the answer?

My point is just this: We cannot combat violence that is provoked by big city social isolation by using reactive defenses like walling off drivers or relying on strong arm tactics like heavy prison sentences to deter such crimes. Believe me, I'm not condoning acts of aggression. In my twenty-year bus driving career, I've been assaulted three times—once by a fellow driver. It certainly was disturbing and I am very sympathetic to the vulnerable position drivers are in. They are simply doing their job, but because they are out in the public, they are occasionally prey to disturbed or unhappy people.

What If...

As the old Chinese proverb says, *"It is better to light a candle than to curse the darkness,"* which is why I believe that a better solution to driver assault is to create a safer environment on buses by altering the environment on the bus from the inside out.

I believe—no, I actually know from years of doing this— that people respond differently when they are treated as human beings worthy of our time, attention and respect. By using the Art of Acknowledgement, we create a sense of connection with our passengers. By making them feel seen and validated simply for being human, we counteract the sense of isolation that is at the source of violence and disconnection.

People are less likely to assault someone who is friendly. People are less likely to assault someone who seems to be surrounded by people who are energetically connected and are having fun. Bystanders are more likely to respond when they feel involved as they do when they are personally addressed. It's not up to just one person, but one person can be the model that gives each of us courage to take a stand.

Overcoming Bystander Effect[1]

A street performer dressed in a toga and painted completely white stood motionless for long periods of time on the steps of Sacre Coeur in Paris. As Michele, my co-writer, and her fifteen-year-old son stood entranced by the living statue, another tourist leaned forward and flicked his lighter setting the edge of the toga on fire. For a horrified moment no one moved or uttered a word. Then Michele jumped forward pulling on the fabric and put out the flames with her hand.

---

[1] **The Bystander Effect**

A phenomenon in which the greater the number of people present, the less likely people are to help a person in distress. When an emergency situation occurs, observers are more likely to take action if there are few or no other witnesses.

There are two major factors that contribute to the bystander effect. First, the presence of other people creates a diffusion of responsibility. Because there are other observers, individuals do not feel as much pressure to take action, since the responsibility to take action is thought to be shared among all of those present. The second reason is the need to behave in correct and socially acceptable ways. When other observers fail to react, individuals often take this as a signal that a response is not needed or not appropriate.

What upset Michele was twofold: First, that someone would set another person alight as a joke; and second, that no one did anything. Everyone stood there frozen, as though they were watching to see the performer's reaction when he finally realized he was on fire.

I, however, see something she missed. I saw in Michele the same qualities you see in heroes. She broke free of the bubble of what is known as Bystander Effect and stepped forward to initiate responsible action coming from a strong sense of what she saw as right. Further to her credit she mirrored humane, caring behaviour to her son and to all those witnessing the event.

It is human nature to want to be like those around us, but our desire to fit in sometimes means that we won't do anything that makes us stand out or attracts too much attention. However, using the Art of Acknowledgement on the job means that I turn strangers into allies, passengers and customers into responsible and pro-active citizens.

Valendation Day

"Excuse me please. I need to see your pass again."

The young student looked worried, stopping in her tracks and staring perplexed at her pass.

"That's right. It's a new policy. I need to Valendate your pass. Thank you." With a quick movement I placed a heart sticker onto her pass. "Happy Valentine's Day!"

Her look of delighted surprise was an absolute joy. All day I played with passengers of all ages and genders, gently slapping hearts onto tickets, jackets or hands. Who would have guessed that for less than three dollars you could have this much fun?

"Thanks for making my day."
"Wow. Look what I got!"
"Hey driver, I'm wearing your heart on my sleeve!"

By the time I got home, I was smiling from ear to ear and ten times more energized than I had been when I had started my shift eight hours earlier. I had 'valendated' over three hundred people on February 14th.

A Tommy T Quip

You're Not Very Bright!

"Nothing personal, but you're not very bright!" I announce loudly over the intercom.

The young man who is boarding stares at me with a stunned look on his face.

"Just in case you want to come up and slap me," I continue, "because you think I am referring to your intelligence. I am not. I simply would like to draw your attention to your dress code. You are all wearing black! Black boots, black pants, black coats, black scarves and to top it all off black hats! I'm sure you'd be a hit on the catwalks of Milan or London, but on the streets of rainy Vancouver after dark your outfit is deadly."

"From where I sit in the driver's seat it is almost impossible to see you. So here's a tip: Brighten Up! Get a small flashlight and wave it towards the traffic as you cross the street. If you're at the bus stop, try this: Wave your cell phone in an arc. That way you can be seen."

A few weeks later another bus driver commented that the passengers on his route were waving their cell phones. I laugh, "That was my old route. Those are my brightest passengers. I guess they finally get it."

Chapter 3
The Art of
Acknowledgement

*"What I do on the bus with my conscious
acknowledgements and kindness is food
for the soul and I see in the passengers'
faces how long they have hungered for it."*
~ Tommy Transit

"**N**ice earrings!"
"I like your brooch."
"Great necklace."
"Nice suit. I didn't know we had a dress code."
"You look sharp. You getting married?"
"You look great. Did you get the job?"
"Nice tie."
"Great shoes."
"Hey, I love what the rain does to your hair."
"Great haircut. Nice colour. Suits you."

Everybody who boards my bus gets a smile, a greeting, a nod, a wave or even, on occasion, a playful wink. Whenever possible, I add a personalized compliment that acknowledges a unique or special quality that I see in them. When there is no time to be specific, I simply say, "Thank-you," or "Good Morning," with a smile as passengers board the bus. No matter how brief the moment, my intention is to make each and every person feel welcome.

It may not seem earth shattering at first, but this *Art of Acknowledgement* was directly inspired by Denis Waitely's quote. It was exactly the right tool that I could use to bring a little kindness into the lives of the hundreds of people who crossed my path daily. And it works like a charm.

This hunger to be seen runs so deep that at every bus stop I have the joy of seeing people light up and come alive just from the simple act of looking them in the eye and giving them a genuine smile or a personalized compliment. I can honestly say that I probably see more smiles in a day than most politicians or rock stars. Not only does this small act of kindness touch my passengers, but it also has quite literally transformed my job. From merely being a shuttling machine, I bring humanity and caring to others. It has spilled over into all aspects of my life, making it magical and joyous and filled with the most wonderful people. I truly feel honoured[2] and blessed.

Practicing the Art of Acknowledgement is simple: I choose something about someone that appeals to me. I always look for the best or sweetest thing about them. Usually it's what first catches my eye: the tilt of a stylish hat, the sparkle in the eye, or a mischievous grin. The key is to find the goodness, because it's always there. If it doesn't come quickly, it makes me aware that the inner naysayers have snuck back into my brain and are trying to control how I view the world. I make a point of not going into a long pre-meditated thinking process; I just articulate the first nice thing I notice. Having seen it, I say it graciously, with conviction and from the heart. I make sure I am being authentic and I never make stuff up...although I like to play with the edges sometimes.

I take myself out of the equation. This is not a time for comparison, I simply am the witness to their unique presence, and I articulate what I see. We all want to be seen, heard and acknowledged in the best light. When this happens, we naturally light up and feel good about ourselves.

---

[2] By the way, as a Canadian, I believe there is no honour without 'u' (you).

Be the Light in the Shadow

Mary Robinson Reynolds, the award winning speaker, author and producer of *The Acknowledgement Movie,* says that there are 7 Top Reasons why we don't acknowledge one another:

1. Jealousy and envy; fear of being seen as insincere flattery, fake.
2. Speechless; as in "ah, don't know what to say," can't find the words.
3. I'll do it tomorrow; tomorrow never comes.
4. That person is so great they don't need it or it'll give them a big (or bigger) head.
5. If you do it too much it will lose its impact and/or importance.
6. Fear of being rejected; blown off. Feeling vulnerable.
7. Don't belong, so why bother.

Mary's "7 Top Reasons" really show how wrong (or unexamined) thinking can rule the roost. In essence they are fear based, negative beliefs that make no practical sense. When we get out of our (dis)comfort zone and take a moment to connect genuinely with another human being, we have no idea where it will take us or how it may affect them. Mary's five-minute movie is a great example of this and well worth watching: www.AcknowledgmentMovie.com

Kick-Starting Change

According to Mel Robbins, (a life and career coach, and syndicated radio and TV personality who helps people get what they want in life), our problem is not a shortage of inspiring ideas. No, the problem is that we don't act on the zillions of inspiring ideas we do get. She describes the brain as having two speeds: autopilot and emergency brake. Most of the time, we act on auto-pilot which doesn't require much effort and keeps us comfortably puttering along through life. Then in the middle of our day we may suddenly get an idea that inspires us. But, if we don't act on that impulse and do something about that idea within five seconds, we've just pulled the emergency brake on ourselves and we won't do it.

The message is: if we really want to make a change in our life, then we can't wait until we *feel* like doing it, because it's unlikely that it's ever going to happen. Imagining that someday we will feel like doing it is a delay tactic the mind employs in order to stay comfortably ensconced in autopilot. So, what does Mel suggest? How can we break out of the rut and do what we said we wanted to do? Simple: set the alarm on your bedside clock for thirty minutes earlier than usual. When it rings tomorrow morning, don't hit snooze alarm (technology's version of autopilot). Don't roll over for just another five minutes. No. Jump out of bed right away and start your day.

By overcoming physical habits, we disrupt the automatic patterns of behaviour. As Mel says, "It's simple, but it's not easy." As humans we hunger for exploration and growth. NOT acting on what we say we want is what leads us to frustration, disappointment, resentment, self-hatred and believing that we are victims of circumstances. According to Mel, it's up to us break the autopilot circuits and kick-start ourselves on the road to realizing our dreams. Now go re-set that alarm clock!

No One Wants to Be Invisible

"Wow you look fantastic," I said, "You'll get that job!"

The sharply dressed young woman, sporting a nervous smile and carrying a briefcase in one hand, looked at me quizzically.

"How did you know I was going to a job interview?"

"No, I'm not psychic. Just a lucky guess. What kind of job do you do and where have you worked?"

"I'm from Nova Scotia and I work in Public Relations in the hospitality industry. I'm heading to the Hotel Vancouver for an interview, which is why I'm feeling a bit nervous."

As I handed her my business card, I wished her good luck at the interview and added, "Email me. I know some people who may be able to help you."

Good job seeker that she was, Cassandra followed up with an email a few days later and I forwarded her several connections at a number of well-established hotels in town. Three weeks later she hopped on my bus, giddily informing me that one of the contacts I suggested had arranged an interview and she was now heading to her first day on the job. I was thrilled for her and had the joy of driving her to work for several months before losing track of her. It's just another way that I personify my mission and 'walk my talk'. It always gives me great joy to be in a position to assist and be of service to others.

A Tommy T Quip

Happy Birthday

"Whoa. Great hat!"
A young woman in her early twenties is sporting a bright pink cowboy hat. "It's my birthday and my friend is taking me to Denny's restaurant," she informs me, "They give free meals on your birthday, you know."

After she sits down, I whisper to others as they board the bus, "How would you like to commit a random act of kindness? Wish the woman in the pink cowboy hat 'Happy Birthday'." About ten of them chose to do just that.

As she leaves, she says, "That's the nicest thing anyone's done on my birthday."
"What about your friend meeting you for dinner?" I remind her.
"Oh, that's a free lunch," she says dismissively.
"That's not the point. It's the thought behind it," I say, "Plus he gets to enjoy your company."

"Hey," she says lighting up, "I'm studying psychology and it just happens that my thesis is about the effects of kindness on others. You'd be perfect to shadow so I can watch how others respond to your kind words."

Chapter 4

No One Forgets How You Make Them Feel

"The fragrance of the rose lingers on the hand of the giver." ~ Hada Bejar

H ey, thanks for picking up supper," I call out to a middle aged woman loaded down with groceries. I expect her to laugh along with me.

Instead she angrily throws back, "Last week someone stole my groceries right off the bus," as though it was my fault that thieves also rode buses. "If I could afford a car, I wouldn't have to take the blasted bus at all. It's such a pain."

"I'm so sorry. Are you willing to have a good experience on the bus, today?"

"Sure, although I can't imagine what that would look like," she snaps back cynically.

"Maybe it would look something like this," I say handing her a long stem red rose. "Happy Valentine's Day. Here's to nicer experiences in your future, especially on the bus."

A huge smile lights up her face as her anger and frustration melts away. She gently whispers, "This is the nicest thing anyone has done for me in a long time. Thank you."

It would have been easy to let the woman remain caught up in her own angry thoughts and cranky mood. It's not like I didn't see it coming. Her entire body vibrated with irritation and disappointment. In her case, I would have been forgiven for jumping to conclusions and assessing her as someone I didn't want to deal with. But that's not my style. Instead, I go out of my way to bring play, fun and smiles onto my bus. Every Valentine's Day, I load up with dozens of roses that I pass out to women who get on my bus that day. The roses always go quickly and put smiles on many faces.

As the expression goes, "You can't judge a book by its cover," but unfortunately, that's exactly what we do all the time. The instant we first catch sight of someone, we immediately judge their appearance: the kind of clothes they wear—how stylishly, conservatively or outlandishly they dress. In a nanosecond we are picking up clues as to their emotional and mental well-being by the way they carry themselves: Are they walking erect and proud, are they dragging their heels or are they wrapped up in their own little world?

I also notice that I instantaneously sum up other people with thoughts about who they are. I call these my three constant inner companions: The Critic, The Cynic and The Judge. While these aspects of my ego are trying to protect me, most of the time they shut me off from seeing who another person really is. It takes a bit of mental shifting to consciously remind myself that I am the chairman of my own board of directors and that when these naysayers start critiquing, being cynical or judging I can tell them that they are not welcome at the meeting. A closed heart cannot see the good in others. What a shame!

Seeing the Soul of Another

"The divine light in me sees the divine light in you." This Sanskrit greeting is not the way we were taught to see each other in our culture, but this is what 'Namaste' means. Even if you ask a native of India, they might say that it means, "Hello," or "How are you?" As Jeffrey Armstrong, a Vedic teacher, says, "The actual word is comprised of three separate words Na-Mas-Te which in English can be translated as "Not - Me - (but) You."

What a refreshing way of seeing our fellow human beings. By looking directly into your eyes, I see your soul. Not your personality, not your social condition, not your choice of fashion, but simply your inner light—absent of any criticism or judgement. This is what I look for when I practice the Art of Acknowledgement.

We all share a hunger for goodness, for love, for joy, but sometimes it can be deeply buried by the pain and difficulties experienced in life. Be assured the light, the good, the unique quality that makes each person different from anybody else on the planet is standing there right in front of you, waiting to be seen. In my experience, people are tickled pink when you find it and remind them of how their unique candle shines.

I like being inventive when I acknowledge someone. I try to notice something that might not at first have been obvious to me. They may be wearing a colourful shirt that I would never hang in my wardrobe, but since this is not about me and they chose the shirt for themselves because they liked it, I use that as an opportunity to complement them on their taste.

"Wow. What a great shirt!"
"Great colour on you."
"Whoa. Got to get my shades on - you're sparkling today."

Voice inflection is important: I always work on keeping it friendly, humorous and playful. I can almost guarantee these exchanges will help others shine and they will feel seen. Often all that is needed is the simple gift of taking a few moments to acknowledge another person's existence and humanity. I make sure that I am sweet with my words. Why? It feels good and I'm pretty sure we all like to feel good. Guess what? They do, too.

Scraped Knees

"Excuse me driver, but did you used to drive the Willingdon Bus in Burnaby?"

I looked up to see a well-dressed woman in her mid-twenties standing beside me, "Well yes I did, but that was a few years ago. Did you take my bus back then?"

"I knew it was you, I recognized that hat of yours, your voice and helpful manner."

"Thank you, that is very cool that you remember. I trust it was a good memory?"

"I was late for school and racing for the bus, you looked up my side street, saw me running and waited at the stop. In my haste I slipped and fell, ripping my knapsack and spilling my books and papers all over the sidewalk. You got off the bus helped me pick everything up, gave me a wet paper towel for my bloodied knee, a plastic bag for my useless knapsack and a transfer because I had lost my ticket. You never made me feel badly for holding up the bus with other passengers on it. I was very grateful and never forgot your kindness."

"Wow, I remember that. You were very upset. That was almost ten years ago. Thank you for coming up and saying hello."

"Actually I was thirteen and I'm twenty-five now and in university, so it's been twelve years."

I was very touched as I realized that people remember how you make them feel for a very, very long time. It's nice to have those memories be good ones.

Wish Me Well

"Could you pray for me?"

I immediately wanted to remind the earnest young man that I was a bus driver and not a priest, but I saw from his worried face that he was very serious. Just a moment ago, he had stepped off the back of the bus and then run at full speed to the front, quickly bounding up the front steps to make his breathless request.

"I respect you as an elder and so I'd really like to ask this favour of you. I write my midterms at the university in two days. Could you please pray for me?"

Oh. Now it was clear. "What mark would you like to get? I inquired.

"Well, my English is not so good, but I have studied hard. I think I can get 70 to 80 percent."

"Okay," I advise, "I want you to see 75% in your mind. Keep studying, but also picture 75%. What time is your exam?"

"2:30 in the afternoon," he replies.

"Good," I tell him, "I'll keep you in my thoughts."

He got off the bus with a big smile and a wave.

I jotted a reminder note about the scheduled time of his exam on a bus transfer that I later transferred into an alarm on my phone. Two days later, the alarm buzzed and while I drove through heavy afternoon traffic, I envisioned him calmly and coolly writing a successful paper.

This is a good example of trusting the energy in the Universe. I saw him again two weeks later and called out, "Hey, I was thinking of you at 2:30 on your exam day. How did it go?"

He smiled happy to be recognized, replying, "I remembered your tip about visualizing the mark I wanted. I pictured 80 and that's exactly what I got. Thanks."

We high-fived each other as he got off the bus.

A Tommy T Quip

Where's My Pass?

Two women hop in. The first one flashes her pass at me and the second opens an enormous floppy purse and scrambles to find her fare. She says to her friend, "Where did I leave my monthly pass?"

I pipe up, "Well the last time I saw it, it was on the counter in the kitchen right by the toaster and your coffee cup."

They look at me stunned. Then all three of us burst into laughter.

While her friend continues to dig through her purse, the first woman says, "So, when was he in your kitchen, Sue?"

Sue gives me a playful wink, "Recently apparently, but we don't want to talk about it." She shoots me a warning look, "Do we?"

"Good plan," I quickly add.
Giggles all round as she triumphantly pulls out a valid pass.

Chapter 5

The Ripple Effect Returns

"A candle lighting another candle loses nothing and the whole world is a brighter place." ~ *Proverb*

The sidewalk is jammed with young people standing around waiting for the next bus. There is no room for anyone to pass. I am wearing my signature hat and the bus company jacket as I move through the crowd, playfully bringing to their attention that they are blocking the way by pointing to the road and the storefronts. "Sidewalk. Roadway. Window shop. Sidewalk. Coming through. Excuse me, please. Thank you. Appreciate that. Thank you kindly, you guys are the best."

They part, laughing and talking. Suddenly one young man calls out, "Hey nice hat."
Another adds, "Love your jacket."
Still another one chimes in, "Great attitude."
More voices add:
"Nice shoes."
"Cool pants, man."
Then a girl calls out, "Hey, how come you're not driving the #41 anymore? We miss you."

I turn and look at them, tears filling my eyes. The year before, I had been driving the #41, a busy route that goes past several schools. During the week, I picked up this same group of well dressed young people. As they boarded the bus, I would acknowledge each of them, my patter sounding something like this:
"Hi, how are you today?"
"Did you get your homework done?"
"Nice earrings."
"Nice boots."
"Love your hair."

"Great smile."

"Hi. Good to see you again. I feel like your personal chauffeur."

A nose stud would get this response: I tap the side of my nose and say, "Looks like one of the sparkles fell out of your eye."

Etc, etc.

I had automatically picked out something that distinguished them from their fellow students. After all, we each like to be seen as individuals, particularly teenagers. Trusting that they had heard me and having no idea what effect, if any, I was having, they smiled and laughed as they got on the bus. I encouraged them to make room for others by saying, "Stuff the bus with bodies, right to the back, thank you. Pretend it's a contest and you are actually winning. That's it, thank you kindly." I did this for three months and then my route changed.

I turned to look at the group of teens standing in front of me full of smiles and hopes, amazed at my serendipitous fortune that conspired to have me be there at just the right moment and be recognized. I was equally astounded that they had remembered me and fed back to me snippets of the acknowledgements I had doled out to them a whole school year earlier.

"You guys are awesome. Good to see you again," I said shaking my head in disbelief, "Thanks for making my day. I hope to drive your bus soon. I miss all of you, too."

Two minutes later they were gone.

I think those seeds I planted in the students may have improved their interactions with their family, teachers and friends. My hope is that this simple art of acknowledging others will add kindness and cut down on bullying.

Planting Seeds

"The true meaning of life is to plant trees
in the shade of which you'll never sit."
- Nelson Henderson

It took me a moment to fathom the depth of my emotional response. Was my ego stroked because this was something I had initiated? Perhaps a little, but then the real significance of their remarks hit me. These young people hadn't been looking for me to show up. Nonetheless, their words had poured forth naturally and easily. Last spring I had planted seeds of kindness and acknowledgement. Today I was witnessing that they had taken root, and I had had the pleasure of wading through the harvest of kindness and goodwill.

One of my boyhood heroes was Johnny Appleseed who wandered through the wilderness in the 18th century planting apple trees across America. He would clear the land by chopping out weeds and brush by hand and planting apple seeds in neat rows, building a brush fence around the area to keep out animals. Somewhere, somehow, he had caught a vision of blossoming apple trees lifting the spirits of early settlers as they struggled to clear the land. Johnny Applessed had an intention of creating something, not for himself or his heirs, but solely that others could enjoy and benefit from for years to come.

People plant trees for many reasons and one of those reasons is to relax in their shade, but wise men create, build and plant for a future that they may never personally benefit from.

The Power of Encouragement

"We cannot hold a torch to light another's path without brightening our own."
~ *Ben Sweetland*

"Hey Tommy, were you speaking with a young East Indian woman on your bus recently? Did you tell her how much you appreciate the years of hard work a musician must go through in order to bring pleasure to others?"

My friend Theda, a voice coach and guitar teacher, was on the phone. It took me a moment, but as I reflected back I remembered that a few weeks earlier I had been announcing 'Thoughts for the day' over the loudspeaker, and the one I had shared was: "It's easy to find help moving the stool when actually it's the piano that needs lifting." A few days later a lovely young woman with jet black hair approached me about the quote I had shared.

"You seem to be very knowledgeable about pianos?" I remarked as we chatted.

"I've been studying piano, guitar and voice," she agreed.

"You must really love music and aren't simply doing it because your folks threaten you with 'No friends' if you don't practice."

She laughed. "I love music and thanks but I don't live at home anymore."

"I've got so much respect for people like you who have the tenacity, strength and discipline it takes to do what you do. I'm the guy sitting in the audience with tears of joy running down my cheeks for the beauty of your music. Let me know when your next performance is so I can come and support you. Keep up the good work. You are amazing. Nice to chat. Goodnight." I gave her my card and she slipped into the night.

Theda spoke up again, "Well, that young woman just happens to be a student of mine who was so frustrated at her progress that she quit her lessons that night. The next day she phoned me saying that when she had left my place she looked for a sign. Then she had met an angel on the bus whose words had inspired her to change her mind. She now wished to continue with the music coaching. Thanks, I knew it had to be you."

Skip forward two years:
"Tommy?" It was Theda on phone again. "Are you up for a visit?"

"Sure." I responded, as we had not seen each other for a while.

After a cup of tea and cookies, Theda insisted we go for a drive. I was a bit mystified as we pulled into the driveway of a large Sikh Temple. Inside I was instructed to don headgear in order to be allowed into the inner sanctuary. Before we moved into the temple, Theda introduced me to a stunning young woman in a glittering sequined sari.

"Do you remember her?" Theda asked.

"No, I don't believe I've had the pleasure," I said shaking my head.

Extending her hand the young woman said, "Two years ago I was ready to quit playing music. But on your bus you spoke to me and your words encouraged me to keep on studying. You also asked to come when I performed. Welcome to my first concert."

My eyes filled with tears as I realized the words I had spoken to her casually, but passionately two years earlier had been the catalyst to this evening. Entering the temple, she joined a small group of musicians on a low stage and sang and played tabla for over an hour. During the performance, a constant stream of men, women and children walked to edge of the stage and tossed money onto the carpet in front of the young woman.

At the end of the concert, she rose and announced proudly, "Two years ago I played at a family wedding and my uncle was so impressed with my voice that he paid for me to study in India for the past two years with a sitar player who had been a student of the great Ravi Shankar. The money you have generously donated will be used to create a bursary at the University of British Columbia for East Indian women to pursue their love of music."

The temple erupted in cheers and clapping. Thankfully, I was seated as I was weak in the knees and silently wept for joy. It was a remarkable example of the ripple effect becoming a tsunami of change.

Downtown Espresso

"Good morning sir, is that my low fat latte with the nutmeg sprinkles?" I say holding out my open hand as he juggles his pass, coffee and briefcase.

Smiling he says, "Maybe next time."

"Perfect, the good news is that I will be here tomorrow at exactly the same time." We both have a good laugh.

The next day he's there like clockwork, with a big smile and two cups. "Good morning" he greets me cheerily passing me a cuppa. "Just the way you like it."

"Wow. That's so nice. Did you know that you are the first person in 18 years to buy me a coffee? I really appreciate your kindness, thank you."

Now every time I see him, even if he is just walking on the street, I honk the horn or call out, "Two sugars, please," which solicits a smile and a wave from him every time. I have never forgotten how good and appreciated I felt when he brought me that simple cup of coffee. The interesting thing is that I don't even drink coffee but I did that day out of sheer appreciation. I have been thanking him for that cuppa for a long time, and every time I do I feel warm inside—warmer than I would even by drinking it.

A Tommy T Quip

Seeing Double!

"Was it fun growing up as twins?" I ask two teenage girls with identically charming eyes.

An older woman comes up to chat after the girls have left. "I enjoyed your conversation with the twins. I'm the mother of twins."

On the same shift a few hours later, Colleen, a passenger I haven't seen for a while, gets on. "How's your day?" she inquires.

I tell her the double story of twins.

She looks at me strangely, then says, "I'm also a twin."

We have funny weather sometimes in Vancouver, but that day it was raining twins.

Chapter 6
Are You Fishing or Farming?

"Oh, the comfort–the inexpressible comfort of feeling safe with a person–having neither to weigh thoughts nor measure words, but pouring them all right out, just as they are, chaff and grain together; certain that a faithful hand will take and sift them, keep what is worth keeping, and with the breath of kindness blow the rest away."
~ Dinah Maria Mulock Craik

"I thought you were flirting with me."

An attractive young woman in her mid twenties is standing beside the fare box looking at me with an intensity that makes me realize this is no joke. I recognize her as a new 'regular' who has been boarding my bus for just over a week. "I recently got married and it bothered me that you might be trying to pick me up."

For once, I am lost for words and cannot remember anything that I might have said to give her this impression. Furthermore, I am old enough to be her grandfather. If I'm not careful, this could go seriously wrong.

Looking over at the young woman as I maneuver the bus around a corner, I reflect that I had probably commented on her lovely head of frizzy auburn hair, but that is the kind of thing I say all the time.

This morning was no different, from my point of view. I had said hello to numerous women; some were young students on the way to school, others old enough to be my mother. I would smile and compliment them on a particularly attractive hat, brooch or shawl. And I compliment men as well. Serious young men dressed in business suits on their way to the office would hear, "All the world loves a sharp dressed man!" In my usual manner, I noticed something about each and every one of my passengers as they clambered aboard.

One exchange in particular had sparked a delightful interaction. As an elderly woman slowly eased her way onto the bus, I remarked, "Your cane is a beautiful work of art. I'll bet there's a story behind that." The bus was absolutely packed with the early morning rush hour crush. The elderly woman sat in the 'chat seat' just behind me and proudly told me that her grandson had found the stick on a Boy Scout hike in the same mountains she had grown up in as a child. He had hand carved it for her.

"You must be very proud of your grandson," I remarked.

With tears of joy in her eyes she gave me a slightly nostalgic smile, "He lives in the Kootenays and I don't see him as much as I would like."

"Thanks. Loved your story," I called to her as she got off the bus.

The young woman who had confronted me spoke again. "When you complimented me every day over the past week I thought you were flirting with me. So this morning I sat behind you and listened as everyone got on the bus. I heard your exchange with the lady with the beautifully carved cane. It was then that I realized that you compliment almost everyone. I watched people's faces light up in response to your words as they got on the bus. Keep up the good work. I am glad I waited and got a second impression." I thanked her for expressing her concerns and congratulated her on her recent marriage as she got off at the next stop.

Hey Guys: New Thought

For most men, it's as difficult to not notice a woman's beauty as it is to not notice a lovely garden of spring flowers or a gorgeous sunset. But I am well aware that my response to a woman's attractiveness must be appropriate and respectful. Commenting on a woman's personal appearance is meant to be a compliment; however, her response will depend entirely on who's doing the noticing. Some men look at a woman as an object of beauty; some as though they'd like to have her over in the evening in the hopes she'll stay for breakfast. Hey guys: new thought. What if we simply looked at women and saw their beauty as a gift to the world? We would then be able to express appreciation in a way that lands sweetly with them.

Before I go any further, let me say it loud and clear so there can be no mistake: I love women. They are beautiful, kind, intelligent, intuitive and engaging. I can't imagine a world without women. Almost all of my friends are women and I enjoy their company. These women are not my 'girlfriends' and yet we go out to parties, concerts and dinners on a regular basis. I'm very clear about the boundaries between appropriate and inappropriate behaviour with women, mostly because they let me know if I'm out of bounds. And because I understand women so well, I also know that in order to maintain their trust, they need to feel safe. If my intentions are mixed, they quickly pick that up.

Most women spend a fortune on their appearance. They take the time to put on their makeup, dress in fashionable clothing and adorn themselves with jewellery. They enjoy looking attractive and feeling good about themselves. And most women appreciate a tastefully phrased compliment letting them know their efforts were worth it. One of life's great pleasures for me is seeing a smile light up a woman's face when I toss them a friendly comment.

Are You Fishing?

Even though I sometimes leave home saying, "See you later, I'm off to flirt, I mean work," what I mean is that I have the privilege of having fun and often playful exchanges with women passengers that sometimes have an edge of flirtation. What keeps it from going too far is that all exchanges are done with reverence, appreciation and always come from the heart with a genuine feeling of absolute respect. And most importantly, there is no agenda.

This got me thinking how the lines between acknowledgement, flirting and harassment can sometimes get blurred. Harassment obviously is unwanted and cannot be tolerated. Flirting, while fun at a social event, is like fishing in the wrong environment as it always comes with a hook. Many women think that men give out compliments solely as bait for a date and are justifiably suspicious about their motives. They recognize right away that there is a hidden agenda and are often wary of all hooks from all men.

Try Farming

Acknowledgement is clean and the purpose is simply to add a little joy and recognition into another person's day. Once an acknowledgement is delivered there should be no strings attached because you are not trying to reel in anything. Your intention should be to simply plant seeds of kindness. You are farming, not fishing. This kind of exchange is clean, safe and appreciated.

If you wish to practice the Art of Acknowledgement and scatter joy and happiness like seeds, you have to do it without expectations, as you can never know for sure whether they will sprout and grow. Like any gardener, you hope that what you do will take root, but you cannot hold onto expectations. When you practice the Art of Acknowledgement, do it with the intention to see another person light up. In all of these activities, keep it pure by making sure there is no hidden agenda. Kind, clean acknowledgement soothes, uplifts and nurtures. So, be playful and always respectful.

When I acknowledge a woman and toss her a compliment, I'm not trying to get something back. It's not like I'm playing a game of tennis and expect the other person to hit the ball back to me every time I make a serve. It's important to give freely without any thought of reciprocation, especially when you are out in public and acting as a representative of a company. Giving is its own reward.

Providing Safety for Women

Women have a natural protective mechanism, which sometimes looks like suspicion and mistrust of unsolicited comments they may get from men they do not know. If you are a man, don't take her rebuff personally and respect her for her desire to keep safe boundaries. Daughters, even more than sons, are taught at a very early age to be cautious: "Don't talk to strangers." "I'll come and pick you up," etc. Naturally parents hope the tools they instill in their girls will protect and keep them safe for all their life. So, don't be surprised when you come up against this barrier of self-protection. Honour it and them and let it go. Don't push or ignore their requests. You will get nowhere by being pushy.

Who Needs Feedback?

As time goes on and I become ever more comfortable interacting with total strangers in a fun and playful manner, I find new ways to do what works for everyone. I am very clear that women need to feel safe before they can trust you. If you say something that seems to be getting the wrong reaction, always be ready to apologize. You don't know her emotional state. You may be feeling playful, but perhaps her relationship just broke up, or she lost her job, or a loved one recently died. While it's true that we all crave attention, we hunger for appropriate caring attention, not ogling, catcalls or inappropriate personal comments.

The message here is the importance of how the compliments and acknowledgements are delivered. You have no control over how they are received. None. So keep your delivery honest and clean. Have every intention to be honest and heartfelt. They will know the difference in a heartbeat. So come from the heart and drive on.

When acknowledging a member of the opposite sex, avoid body parts except for hair, eyes and smiles. "My you have the most beautiful eyes. Have a great day," is usually received well. Sometimes a mother will come in with her kids and I will notice that they both have amazing eyes or hair. I look directly at the child and say,

"Wow, it looks like beautiful eyes runs in the family." NEVER, ever look in the rear view mirror to check their reaction. That is you looking for a response.

Younger women may misunderstand my complimentary nature and wonder if I'm a dirty old man hitting on someone young enough to be my daughter (or granddaughter). Because of the time frame—a couple of seconds per person—my remarks are usually short and simple. I'm simply letting them know they've been seen and appreciated:
"Cool hair."
"Nice necklace."
"Snazzy jacket."
"Great nose stud," as I tap my own nose and give them the thumbs up.

Some older women are comfortable enough with themselves that they will flirt back. Even though the bus is literally a pick-up machine, be clear that it is NOT your personal pick-up machine. You are on the job and so you must respond with caution. Keep things light and playful.

The Matchmaker
"Where are you from?"

"From Paris," the young woman replied in a strong French accent.

"Welcome to Vancouver. How are you enjoying your visit?"

"Well, I was hoping to meet a nice young man, but...." her voice trailed off and I could pick up the wistful tones.

As the trolley bus rattled through the busy downtown area, she seemed relieved to have someone to chat with. People come from all over the world to visit Vancouver, but the glow of romance quickly sours when you find yourself alone in a city without any friends.

I immediately wished I could change her visit in a positive happy way. Then within eight blocks, a young French Canadian lad hopped on and asked me a question. Recognizing his accent, I immediately introduced him to the lonely young French woman. They happily chatted away and after a five-minute conversation on the bus I overheard him ask her out for lunch. She willingly agreed, squeezing my arm and flashing me a huge grin as they got off the bus together. Ah young love. I wonder how it went.

A Tommy T Quip

The Sparkle

Nose studs have become very popular in the past few years. I catch the person's eye as they board and tapping the side of my nose I say, "Nice touch."

If time allows I'll add, "Looks like one of the sparkles fell from your eye."

This always gets a huge smile.

Chapter 7
A Job to Love

*"Success is nothing more than going from one
failure to another with undiminished
ENTHUSIASM." ~ Winston Churchill.*

I peered into a dark room, lit only by the lights over a pool table. It was the week after Christmas and I had just been laid off from my job as a cable installer. (Did Jim Carrey get my job?) The country was going through an economic slump and the job market was even damper and grayer than the Vancouver weather.

The sign emblazoned above the door read, 'Transit Club'. A few heads lifted from the game as I inquired, "What does it take to join?"

"You have to be a member of transit or know someone who is," one of them called back.

"Ha. I don't even know a bus driver," I chuckled sardonically.

"Well, you do now. Hi, my name is Terry," a broad hand extended my way and I looked up into a smile that was even broader. That was the start of a whole new way of life.

I was soon playing darts and pool on a regular basis with drivers, supervisors and technicians. "Hey Tom, they're hiring new drivers. You should apply," one of my new pool buddies mentioned as I leaned over to break the rack several months later. I enjoyed spending time at the club and the transit guys were a likeable bunch. I also knew that the wages were substantially better than my previous jobs and the benefits were very attractive. I sure could use a steady position and I loved driving. It looked like the perfect opportunity for me.

Bright and early the next day, I stood in line at head office with my application papers and resume in hand. "Thank-you for applying," said the clerk. I went home eagerly awaiting a callback. Weeks later the response was...nothing.

Back at the club I overheard two drivers commiserating, "Did you hear they've had over three thousand applicants for only twenty-five driver positions?" This news hit me like a punch in the stomach. How was I to get this well paying job if there were so many applicants ahead of me? It looked like it was going to be easier to jump in front of a bus than it would be to get into the driver's seat. I could slump into a deeper depression or...I could hatch a cunning plan.

Persistence Pays

Monday morning found me back at head office filling out another application. I signed it and slipped it into the box on the front desk. I repeated this on Tuesday, and again on Wednesday. Thursday and Friday as well. Thank goodness they were closed on Saturday and Sunday as I was now suffering from writer's cramp. Monday rolled around and I was back like a bad penny. The letters began to roll in thanking me for taking the time to apply. I got similar letters on Tuesday, Wednesday, Thursday and Friday. I called Personnel to thank them, adding, "Please save our forests. You don't need to send me any more letters as I will be applying again tomorrow."

I showed up every workday for three full weeks: a total of twenty-one days, twenty-one resumes and twenty-one application forms. I was getting to know the staff on a first name basis. "Morning Tom," they called out assuming I worked there.

"Oh no, I don't work here. Not yet. See you tomorrow".

At the end of three weeks I sensed the office staff were tiring of me. Maybe they would fire me before I even got the job. I gave us all a week off and helped a friend paint his house.

Monday came as did I with new tactics. This time I put in a phone call to Kim, the person I knew who was doing the hiring. I did this for about two weeks until I could hear the annoyance in her voice. "It's easy. Hire me and the calls will end," I suggested, "Then, stay off my bus," I added. Kim laughed even as she heaved another deep sigh. "Just call once a month," she countered, "And I will let you know where you stand." I realized that although I had been calling regularly she still didn't know who I was. Of course she had heard me announce my name when I called, but she was also busy trying to process the other 2,999 applications. I needed to do something to stand out from the crowd.

The following day I disguised my voice, "Hi, can you tell me when Kim has her lunch? I'm an old friend and haven't seen her for years. I'd like to surprise her."

"Who can I say is calling," chirped the receptionist mechanically.

"Well it wouldn't be much of a surprise if she knew, now would it?" I responded.

For the next three weeks I targeted my phone calls to match Kim's lunch break when I knew she'd be away from her desk. Three times a week she received a voice message of me slowly spelling my name and phone number. At the end of the three-week period, I put in a call to Kim before coffee break when I knew she would still be at her desk. "Have you been ignoring my messages?"

"Oh," she laughed recognizing my voice, "This must be Tom."

Bingo! My strategy worked. She now knew who I was. We had a giggle and as a courtesy my calls dropped to monthly check-ins.

On the first Monday of March I put in another call, "Hey Kim, want to go out for coffee?" She declined.
The first Monday of April: "How about lunch?"

She rejected my offer.

May's call included flowers, "Where can I send them?"

"Not necessary, Tom," she replied laughing. By this point she was looking forward to my light-hearted calls as a break from the office routine.

Six months from the day I had first walked into the personnel office, I received a call for an interview. Tests, forms and training kept me busy for the next six weeks. The end of the training culminated in a celebratory brunch at head office with the heads of all the departments in attendance. As we twenty successful new recruits enjoyed tea, coffee, muffins and crumpets, I spotted the nametag of the woman sitting beside me.

"Kim!" I exclaimed with a smile. I turned to her and started counting on my fingers, "You turned me down for coffee. You turned me down for lunch. You turned away my bouquet of flowers. I'm delighted to finally share a muffin with you today. But," I added in mock seriousness, "Remember to stay off my bus!"

She laughed and said, "Oh my gawd, you've got to be Tom."

It seems Dad was right: The squeaky wheel does get the grease. That persistence, that drive to get what I want, has allowed me to live a bigger life. It's given me the chance to make an impact on hundreds of thousands of passengers every day. I didn't see that possibility in the job description.

I love my job so much that it always takes me by surprise when others say how much they dislike what they do.

A Tommy T Quip

Enthusiastic Appreciation

"Nice shirt."
A mentally challenged young man in his late teens is a frequent passenger. Overweight and extremely shy he never speaks or looks at me. However, when I acknowledge him about his shirt, he smiles.

"Cool hat," I say to him a few days later when I see him again. Today as he is about to leave he shuffles to the front door so that I will be sure to see him wave back to me as he heads off to his destination.

He steps away to let others board waving his arm vigorously. His simple, authentic enthusiasm and genuine excitement to make certain that I notice him really gives me energy.

Chapter 8
Loving the Job You Have

"Your playing small doesn't serve the world. There's nothing enlightened about shrinking so that other people won't feel insecure around you. We are all meant to shine, as children do. We were born to make manifest the glory of God that is within us. It's not just in some of us; it's in everyone. And as we let our own light shine, we unconsciously give other people permission to do the same. As we are liberated from our own fear, our presence automatically liberates others."
~ Marianne Williamson

"Where's your lovely smile today?"

I was standing in line, waiting for my slice of pizza and pop. The young man behind the counter looked bored and glum. I certainly could identify with his frustration. He probably had a university degree, but here he was serving pizza for minimum wage. He shrugged and rolled his eyes as he responded, "I just started and I've got ten hours yet to go." The exhaustion for hours he hadn't yet worked were etched all over his face.

"You're working those hours anyway," I smiled sympathetically.

He didn't say anything, but a few minutes later as I stood munching on my pizza, he turned to me saying, "How is your day going?" He looked visibly lighter and I could see that the next ten hours were not going to be as arduous as he had thought a few minutes earlier.

Unfortunately there's an epidemic of people who would rather be doing just about anything other than what they are doing, and it always takes me by surprise when I hear people say:
"My job sucks."
"I hate my boss,"
"My coworkers are idiots."
"The pay is terrible."
"It's just a job."
"It pays the bills."
"I'm living for the weekend."

"I can hardly wait 'til I retire."

"Thank God, it's Friday."

And then there's the bumper sticker: "I am not in a hurry, I am on my way to work."

I remember early on in my bus driving career hearing another driver say, "I just drive garbage around all day." He was referring to his passengers - other human beings - as garbage! I was shocked. As a newbie this was hardly the mentoring I needed for my hard won position as a bus operator.

Most work dissatisfaction has little to do with the actual job and everything to do with our thoughts about the job. The unexamined inner attitude behind our negative words usually is, "I shouldn't have to do this," while the real truth is, "I need this job so I can pay my way." All 'hate my job' thoughts are like arguing with reality, and while no one on their deathbed ever uttered, "I wish I'd spent more time at the office," the truth is that we all have to do something to earn our bacon.

To me the choice is obvious: I can either go to work resentfully wishing fate had dealt me an easier hand, or I can allow joy to seep into my life no matter what it is that I do.

Tourist Trap

"Why do you act so happy and friendly with people you don't even know and will never see again?" One of my fellow drivers at the terminus took a long drag on his cigarette eyeing me with bemused contempt. He had been watching my lengthy interaction with a group of tourists who had just got off my bus in Stanley Park. I had been heading towards the washroom when they had asked me directions to the Aquarium and where they could rent bicycles to tour the park. I had joked and chatted with them giving the kind of information and tips that a Vancouverite and bus driver would know. I wished them a pleasant visit as they thanked me and walked away cameras and fanny packs swaying.

"I just can't wait to get them off my bus so I can have a smoke and take some time to myself. " He rolled his eyes in derision, "I don't understand you at all."

"Do you really want an answer?" I queried.

"Sure!"

"It's pretty simple. They have just spent a small fortune travelling thousands of miles to enjoy a holiday in our city. They contribute to our economy in a variety of ways: staying in hotels, eating in restaurants, taking tours, paying for attractions and sites of interest as well as seeing the city by riding our buses. I am part of their experience. I can either be a pleasant part or a frustrating part."

"Bus drivers are a pretty safe bet to go for information. We are knowledgeable about the city and how to get around it. So I choose to do what I would appreciate if I were in their shoes or in their city. Every morning I remember that I have a choice, so I choose to be happy because I don't particularly like the alternative. See you later, have a good shift, but only if you choose to."

Beware the Whiny Virus

When you first applied for your current job, you probably dressed your best for the interview. You handed in your application and resume with the hope that you had all the qualifications they required. You waited expectantly for the call back and when you got word that you were hired, you exultantly called your friends and family with the good news. The first day you got up early to prepare for the new job. All went well for weeks, months or maybe years, but eventually you succumbed. Like the flu and common cold you caught a highly contagious disease from your fellow workers: The Whiny Virus.

This virulent infection is rampant in lunchrooms, around the water cooler and other places that employees gather. Even though we know that this infection is toxic, we want to fit in with our peers and fellow workers, so if they complain we tend to join in. Our initial enthusiasm for the work we do becomes tarnished as we listen to long time employees who seem to get a perverse satisfaction from 'disillusioning' younger and newer staff.

Let's be honest. We all complain about something. Heavens, newspapers, TV and radio are full of hundreds of things to be upset about. Yet what are we hoping to gain by complaining? Do we think the situation will automatically change when we voice our dissatisfaction? Do we enjoy belittling our bosses? Are we looking for solidarity from our fellow grumble-mates? There is nothing inherently wrong with commiserating with our fellow workers, but just as we take precautions not to get infected from sick people, we need to be careful about the thoughts we allow into our minds when we share a "glass of whine" with others.

What is the antidote to passing on or catching a virus that does not support us to feel good about our job? It all boils down to attitude and intention. To rephrase the old Crosby, Stills, Nash and Young song: "If you can't do the job you love, love the job you do."

A Tommy T Quip

What's In Your Pocket

A woman walks past the fare box saying, "He's paying. The tickets are in his pocket."

I look at the man following and say, "She knows what's in your pockets?"

"Yeah, I'm not sure that's a good thing," he replies shaking his head.

"Maybe you could change your pants? Better yet, don't wear any. That'll confuse her."

"Yeah," he grins, "That might confuse a lot of people."

Chapter 9

Buses Run on Diesel, What Fuels You?

"Be the change you want to see in the world."
- Mahatma Gandhi

"**A**re you on drugs?"

"Yes," I reply, enjoying their look of shock, "And I make them myself. Want me to show you how to make your own?" I shoot them a big grin, "Gee, I feel them coursing through my veins as we speak."

I am often so playful and out there as I interact with others on the bus that people sometimes wonder what gives me my extra bounce. I quickly go on to clarify that I'm talking about endorphins. "They are not addictive and I use them because they make me feel good. I highly recommend them to people of all ages."

After a day of acknowledging and interacting with others, I am more energized and full of good spirits than at the beginning of my shift. I literally feel filled up with joy, fun and good will. Life seems blessed and people often remark how I am like the energizer bunny: I keep going and going and going.

So it makes me wonder: if it's true that kindness costs nothing, why are we so often stingy doling it out? Kindness is, by its very nature, generous. In fact, kindness pays HUGE dividends. Not only does it feel good to the person we've been kind to, it turns out that kindness is also very kind...to us. And how do I ensure I have a steady flow of these feel-good drugs? Rather than waiting for chance circumstances to make me feel happy, I've become a drug pusher.

Endorsing Endorphins (and Other Drugs)

A steady flow of morphine-like chemicals are created in the brain that make us feel calmer, more centered and focused no matter what kind of stressful events might be happening around us. Perfect for bus drivers, I figure.

The following drugs are ones I recommend and try to use every single day. We get them in one of two ways: one, they are created when we experience positive events, or two, we can create the circumstances that generate their production. In other words, this drug manufacturer is an inside job. Here's a list of my favourites:

1. When we commit acts of kindness, we get what is known as the **Helpers' High**, a euphoric feeling as our brain pumps out **endorphins**. The more we get (or create), the happier we are! Want even more? Try exercising. It produces a **Runner's High**. So if we act kind while we're jogging, we're likely to get sky high.

2. Smiling also releases endorphins. I smile even when I don't necessarily feel like it. I do it intentionally - smiling a smile that reaches all the way to my eyes...for at least five minutes. Let me know if that works for you. Smile, I mean really SMILE! You know you can do it!

3. **Oxytocin** known as the cuddle hormone plays an important role in romantic love as well as the capacity to feel empathy and trust. So go cuddle your kid or kitty and savour the tasty hormones.

4. Compassion appears to slow inflammation which is what ages us.

5. Go ask for the love and support you need. Feeling that one is cared for and supported by others

creates a feeling of being safe and soothed, whereas feeling uncared for is linked to mental and physical problems.

6. Feeling bad that you're poorer than you wish you were? Well, take heart because you've got more heart. According to studies, the poor are more attuned to suffering, and quicker to express compassion than the affluent. If you're rich, open your heart to those less fortunate than yourself. It'll do you a world of good.

7. Volunteers live longer! Go help out and be here for years to come. I volunteer for Canuck House in Vancouver, a hospice for kids. These kids are incredible. Guess what I do? Drive a bus of course. A busman's holiday right in town.

8. Meditation, prayer, positive visualization or going for a walk in nature will up the **Serotonin** levels that give us that happy feeling, allow us to sleep more soundly, reduce anxiety and depression and boost self esteem. I'm a big yoga fan and get to a class almost every morning.

9. **Dopamine** brings bliss and pleasure. How do you get more? Sex and orgasms. Nothing dopey about that.

10. High levels of bliss and infatuation come to us courtesy of **Phenylethylamine** (say that 5 times without stumbling). Also found in chocolate, which is why it is linked to love.

11. Regulate the body clock with a dollop of anti-aging. **Melatonin** brings its relaxing and recuperative powers whenever we get a good night's sleep.

12. I find it pretty hard to feel anxious, angry, or sad when I'm doubled over in laughter. So have a

good laugh to reduce pain, get rid of negative stress and boost the immune system.

13. Of course a good way to produce a lot of these brain drugs is through a healthy diet. No wonder I love my salads so much!

Now, I know that a kind act releases endorphins in me and that it also releases endorphins in the person I've been kind to. What really blows my mind is that there is evidence that endorphins are released in anyone even watching a kind act. Win-win-win. No war on drugs here.

This is why I seldom let an act of kindness I see go unnoticed. If someone stoops to pick something up that got dropped, I thank them for their kindness. If it happens on the street and not on the bus, I like to toot the horn and give them the thumbs-up and a nod of acknowledgement. They usually 'get' my thank-you. The immediacy of the acknowledgement provides instant positive feedback. Not that they need my approval, but it extends the community of good will into a world that badly needs it. Love, kindness and self-created drugs do indeed make the world a better place.

Maintaining Energy Hour After Hour

Every day before heading out on my shift, I stand in my kitchen reading the sign held up by fridge magnets. Then in a loud voice I call out:

> *Unable to imagine a future,*
> *Imagine a future better than now,*

Us creatures weeping in the abattoir only make noise and do not transform a single fact.
So stop crying. Get up. Go out.
Leap the mossy garden wall, the steel fence or whatever the case may be and crash through painted arcadias, fragments of bliss and roses decorating your fists.

As I reach the last line, my voice rises with the life affirming vigor of the poem and I lift my arms into the air forming a victory 'Y' high above my head. Have I completely lost my mind? Will my housemate call for the boys in the white coats? Nope. The rousing words are part of a daily ritual I use to get myself energized and excited about the day ahead. This poem was part of an incredibly creative program called Poetry in Transit that is funded by the Canada Council for the Arts. No longer relegated to obscure small press editions or dark coffee house slams, poetry is now enjoyed by commuters on buses and subway cars across the country. Reading poetry aloud is one of the tools I use on the job and put into what I call my Count My Blessings Toolbelt that I strap on at the start of each workday.

A Tommy T Quip

Good Incentive to Quit!

A woman at a bus stop in front of a hair salon is taking the last drag on her cigarette. Her hair is covered in metal foil strips. She is clearly in the middle of a hair colouring treatment and has to leave for a while.

As she boards, I say playfully, "Yikes! If that's what smoking does to your hair, I'm quitting today!" She laughs surprised that I noticed she had been smoking.

Chapter 10
The Count My Blessings Toolbelt

"The greatest gift that you could ever give to another is your own happiness, for when you are in a state of joy, happiness, or appreciation, you are fully connected to the Stream of pure, positive Source Energy that is truly who you are. And when you are in that state of connection, anything or anyone that you are holding as your object of attention benefits from your attention." - Esther Hicks (The Abraham Teachings)

The Highest Thought

"Okay," I said to myself, "Take a deep breath."
It was Thanksgiving Day and I was reluctantly at the wheel when I would have much preferred to be sleeping in like the rest of the city on this rainy holiday. The traffic crawled through Chinatown and out to the mega shopping mall in Burnaby. I was not my usual talkative self and noticed I had little tolerance for slow passengers. Over the course of the past hour, I had snapped crankily at confused tourists who didn't have the correct fare and was sarcastic with those perplexed on how to fit the ticket into the fare box. In addition, my break was quickly evaporating with all the delays. Why was everyone in such cheery holiday spirits while I had to work? My mood was becoming more sour by the minute.

"Bus driver on a mission. Ha! What mission? To be as grouchy as possible?"

Only a few years ago I had made a declaration to myself to use my job to consciously make a difference in the lives of my passengers. And yet, here I was sulky, cantankerous and resentful. Being a bus driver is a challenging job and sometimes I am not always the bright, positive light I aspire to be.

I took another deep breath. "Ah. Okay, my energy is low. That's just how it is," I reminded myself shaking off the negative thoughts in an effort to shift my inner state. "Smile, Tommy, smile," I told myself. And then I slowly forced myself to smile. Not a huge big grin, just a quiet little smile to people as they boarded the bus. Within ten minutes I started to notice how only cheery and gracious people were getting on the bus. It was a reminder to me that if I want a change in my world, I have to be the change.

"You are very kind, driver. Your passengers always look happy to be on your bus," an elderly woman remarked. "Have a nice day and try not to work too hard. Bye. See you again," and with a broad smile she exited waving her bag-laden arms.

I immediately felt lifted. Her positive feedback was just the extra boost I needed to keep going. It's miraculous what a few kind words can do. I was grateful for her gentle words to helping me shift away from my dark state, and yet what initiated the energy shift was my inner resolve to serve a higher purpose and 'reach for the higher thought' that had surfaced even through my fatigue. Simply being aware of my intention appeared to have had an impact on the people who subsequently got on my bus. Was I really picking up friendlier, more agile passengers? No. My energetic atmosphere had shifted and consequently I was radiating a more welcoming, friendlier signal that was instantly picked up by the passengers.

I recently stumbled over the fact that about 2,000 thoughts flit through our minds in an hour. Normally, I have a tough time juggling more than one thought, so 2,000 is literally mind boggling. So, it's very easy to let our thoughts rule us instead of directing ourselves into the 'headspace' we wish to occupy. If we can only go as high as our thoughts, then when we get caught up in our daily miseries, anxieties and rehashing old slights, we literally get lost, get pulled down into negativity and forget that we have a choice. Having an intention or 'higher thought', is like a lightning rod that connects me to a larger picture than just my little worries and my little world. It gives me perspective and the choice to live a happier life.

The Attitude of Gratitude

> *Every aspect of our lives grows*
> *richer as we give thanks for what*
> *we have, and what is yet to come.*

The moon hangs over Mount Baker like a giant orange as I drive over the Granville Bridge. It takes my breath away. I look back at the passengers reading their newspapers and dulled by their day. I pick up the intercom: "Ladies and gentlemen, we interrupt your pleasant ride this evening for an amazing event. Off to your left, the full moon over one of the most beautiful cities in the world. You guessed it - Vancouver."

When I slow down at the next bus stop, I slip my hand into my pocket and feel the cool, rounded surface of a small stone. Its smooth surface is painted with a Haida image of a hummingbird that was blessed by a native elder and given to guests at a friend's wedding. This stone is my gratitude stone and I use its gentle weight as a literal 'touch stone', reminding me how grateful I am to be alive. It can also be an anchor to reach for the higher thought in any situation. Often it's the tiniest things that move me to gratitude: a couple holding hands, a freshly painted mural on a downtown wall, a baby cooing and laughing, a dog waiting patiently at a crosswalk until he gets a signal from his owner.

All these things remind me of how grateful I am to be alive. However, the step before gratitude is awareness. For this I thank the Coast Mountain Bus Company. Most driver training programs teach people to read the road from curb to curb, whereas CMBC teaches its drivers to expand their view to encompass building front to building front. Using a wider vision allows you to include the person who bolts from an office door to run between parked cars or to anticipate the actions of a pre-occupied mother pushing a stroller with a crying toddler in tow. As a driver, you never know what might happen, but it's essential to always be on the watch.

Not only does this much wider horizon make me a better driver, but in the process I find that I notice and enjoy all the pleasant and heart-warming activities that are constantly happening on the street I might otherwise miss: a woman loading balloons and a birthday cake into the trunk of her car, a couple walking hand in hand staring into each other's eyes, a piece of whimsical art, a hug on the street, a man pulling his suitcase and stopping to take a picture of the sun reflecting off the city towers. Each of these snapshots of life bring me a surge of joy, but only because I noticed them.

Nature also inspires gratitude as I catch a glimpse of the snow-capped mountains rising behind the city or a glorious sunset splashing the sky in hues of orange and purple. For each of these I silently express my thanks to the Universe for the joys that surround me.

I also am aware every day of how grateful I am for the passengers who ride my bus. First, each and every one of them contributes to my livelihood. Yes, even the freebies. If no one were waiting at bus stops, then there would be no job for me. Second, you have probably concluded from this book that I genuinely love interacting with people and so I am grateful that I have a job where I can connect with others as much as I do...and still get paid. Psst. Don't tell my supervisor.

Emergency Love

"Pass the soy sauce please," Michele asks me while we are sitting in our favourite Chinese Restaurant on Broadway. "Wheeee-oooooo!" the siren pierces the night and I fall quiet closing my eyes. It's very early days in our relationship, and when I open my eyes a moment later I am staring directly into her perplexed expression.

"Someone is not having as good a night as we are," I clarify, "I stopped to send them, their family and friends some healing light. I also express my appreciation for the emergency personnel who are trained and rush to their help."

Michele stared back at me in wonder and awe, "Oh my gosh, I hadn't even noticed the ambulance until you mentioned it."

We tend to tune out emergency vehicles unless we are driving and have to pull over. It usually eludes us that they are there not to annoy or slow us down; they are a luxury. Imagine a world without such a service that in an instant races out to help people in crises. Instead of getting frustrated at missing a green light, we can instead shift our attention to the people who may be facing the worst day of their lives, or the human organ in an ice cooler being rushed to extend someone's life.

I learned this shift in attitude from a remarkable six-month program called HeartMath that was offered privately by a driver who wanted to help her fellow drivers deal with the many stresses of the road. I have since made it an integral tool for responding to challenging situations both on and off the job. The Vancouver Police Department has been trained in this technique as have thousands of schools, educators, health professionals, military personnel, their families and veterans. HeartMath provided us with the tools, technology and training to help us reduce stress, self-regulate emotions and build resilience for healthier, happier lives.

As a driver, I'm on the road everyday and come across many situations that require more than the standard bus driving skills. They require more than quick thinking or fast reflexes. They require heart. Now, whenever I hear the sound of a siren, I immediately visualize my heart glowing with a healing white light that grows brighter and brighter by the second as though it matches the sun's radiance. Then I imagine that light shooting out from my heart and wrapping itself all around me from my toes to the tips of what little hair I have left on my head. I suppose if you could see this it would look a bit like the Michelin Man with energy wrapped around me like thick ropes of white toothpaste or a long pool noodle.

This energetic cocoon empowers and protects me first. Then I aim the imaginary glowing coil of light out towards the emergency vehicle and send blessings to the injured person, the driver and other attendants. I send out the healing white light asking that all involved be given the strength and guidance to get through this time of struggle. I have no idea of what has happened, yet I am very clear that my positive intention of love, strength, healing and gratitude are headed in the right direction. In addition to everything else, it keeps me calm and less stressed with my own resources available should I need to do something actively to help. This is all done in a nanosecond.

If everything, as the physicists are now saying, is energy then we choose what type of energy we wish to express into the world: good or bad, positive or negative. I may not understand it fully, but I am clear that using this tool on the job brings "Emergency Love" into the world, affecting me and everyone else at a time when calm and care is urgently needed.

Manifesting Magic

> *Use whatever excuse you can to vibrate in harmony with those things you've been saying you want. And when you do, those things that are a vibrational equivalent flow into your experience in abundance. Not because you deserve it, not because you've earned it, but because it's the natural consequence of the Law of Attraction. That which is like unto itself is drawn.*
> *- Esther Hicks (The Abraham Teachings)*

Yes, I believe in magic. No, not asking passengers to pick a card when stuck in traffic or making a tiger vanish in a puff of smoke or sawing a woman in half (that's just cruel). The kind of magic that I believe and practice is called the magic of manifestation. Manifestation, also known as The Law of Attraction, is the act of seeing or visualising something and then making it become reality. Don't believe me? Curious for a clear example of this magic? No problem. Let's start out small. How about elastics?

I was driving my car and noticed pens and pencils scattered on the passenger seat from cleaning out the glove box the day before. I thought that an elastic band would be perfect to keep them all together. As I approached my destination on a busy street with very few parking spots, I pulled up behind a woman getting into her car anticipating that she would soon pull out. Instead she chatted on her cell and played with her hair in the mirror.

My first response was irritation as she was not moving for my convenience. Then, rather than getting hooked in, I simply smiled to myself as I witnessed my automatic reaction. I remained unattached to any expectation. I then noticed a car slip out into traffic a few parking spaces ahead providing me with a spot up the street. As I fumbled to pay the meter, I dropped a quarter and bending down to pick it up I saw two elastic bands by the dropped coin. Smiling, I looked heavenward and silently thanked the universe for supplying me once again with twice as much as what I needed.

It is very important to note two things here: First, I have faith that all things are provided and life is fundamentally good. Second, I had shown no ill will towards the woman that was sitting in her car safely using her phone, so my energy remained clean and unattached to the outcome. Upset tends to cloud my vision and that's when I miss things like alternate parking spaces or other options. In this case, it was as if the universe was telling me to wait a minute so that it could guide me to the meter where the elastics I needed were waiting. Cool!

What's that you say? Balderdash? Poppycock? Are you thinking this was just a coincidence and the only magic I was experiencing was magical thinking? Well, I understand how you might mistake it for that. Yet, I challenge you to shift your perspective for a moment and allow another possibility to light up your life as it's lit up mine.

We all have had moments when someone phones just as we were thinking about them. This happens far too frequently to be explained away as simply coincidence. Serendipitous experiences may be our unconscious ability to manifest what we want. Like any muscle, increasing our focused intentions seems to increase the frequency of positive results.

Witness: Within two minutes of having the thought that I need to get myself new driving gloves, I turned the corner in the heat of rush hour traffic and found a pair of brand new fingerless driving gloves in the middle of the road lying forty feet apart from one another. They still had the $45 price tag on them. Very cool!

Okay, you liked that one didn't you? Let's go for something a little bigger, and just for fun let's do a bit of manifesting for someone else. Lindsay, a street musician who regularly gets on my bus was telling me about her frustration around the permits, costs and rules of being a busker. Six minutes later and while still chatting with her, I saw a woman running across a parking lot towards the bus between two stops.

Since I was at a red light and close to the curb, I flipped open the door to let her on the bus. She leaned against the front rail searching for her transit pass while Lindsay and I continued our conversation. As she showed me her pass, the woman said, "Excuse me, but I am on the Buskers Board of Directors for Vancouver this year." We all looked at each other incredulously and I introduced Lindsay while handing them a pad and pen to exchange numbers. I just can't make this stuff up. How is that not a form of manifesting magic? One minute either way, and these two women would never have met.

Here's one more example that occurred just a few months before I retired. My route leads through one of Vancouver's most notorious intersections. On this particular day I noticed that someone had put a paper plate with some Christmas shortbread cookies beside a fellow who had been sleeping on a sidewalk heat vent for several weeks. Musing about whether I should hop out and add a sandwich from my lunch to the plate, I was startled from my reveries by the horn of the bus behind me reminding me that the signal light had turned green. I drove away thinking that what the man on the street really needed was a blanket.

Three blocks and four minutes later, I came to the end of my route where part of the routine is to check the coach for lost items. As I came to the back of the bus, I could hardly believe my eyes. For the first time in my twenty years of driving a bus, I saw before me a clean, folded gray flannel blanket lying on the rear seat. I threw my hands to the sky in disbelief...well, actually in gratitude. While it's true that the city had a campaign to hand out blankets to the homeless and this was probably one of them, I found it hard to believe that it was simply coincidence. For me, it was another example of the magic of manifestation. And, in less time than it's taken to tell you this story, I had placed the blanket over his sleeping body on my return trip.

Manifesting magic is so much fun, and yet it is not always about manifesting something for me. It is also about my deep desire to serve others.

Even though my personal experience is based on my work as a bus driver (transit operator please), the various tools I use are applicable anywhere and at any time for all kinds of jobs. Not only are they great tools for the workplace, but they will enhance your personal life as well.

In addition to the Art of Acknowledgement, these are the tools I always have at hand in my Count My Blessings Toolbelt:
1. The Highest Thought
2. The Attitude of Gratitude
3. Emergency Love
4. Manifesting Magic

A Tommy T Quip

Cute Bike!

I am loading at a stop in front of a gas station.
I notice a very tall man kneeling down and
pumping air into the tires of a tiny pink bicycle
complete with a teddy bear basket and colourful streamers flowing from the handlebars.

I toot the horn catching his attention.
"Didn't they have one in your size?" I call out.
"No," he responds laughing, "But don't you
like the colours!"
"Very nice touch" I add before closing the
doors.
Passengers laugh aloud sending ripples of
merriment throughout the bus.

Chapter 11
Averting Conflict

*"When you argue with reality, you lose,
but only 100% of the time."*
– Byron Katie

"**H**ey driver I got no more money, I musta drank it all. Can you get me back to New West?" A fellow staggered up the steps loudly professing his inability to pay his fare.

Ah, my moment of reckoning. I recall my days of going through the interview process when I first started with transit. "What do you think of drunks?" was tossed at me like a curve ball. At the time I thought it a rather peculiar question, but quickly realized that in our line of business we would undoubtedly be picking up a fair share of inebriated passengers. This is a good thing. Having been a bartender in a previous job, I was familiar with people who take the pleasure of a drink too far. To tell you the truth, I'd prefer to have them on the bus rather than driving on the road around me.

Of course, the inquiry really was, "How are you going to handle someone who gets on your bus in an intoxicated state?" I knew that I'd have to develop a high tolerance level for foolish and drunken behaviour especially if I was going to drive the late night shifts downtown.

"What are you willing to do in exchange?" I throw out playfully. I always find that humour goes a long way in avoiding unpleasantness.

"I could entertain!" he said collapsing onto a seat near the front of the bus and throwing his legs up on another seat as though he was home waiting for his next beer.

"Oops!" I instantly regretted my request. Letting him on without a word would have been so much easier. I wondered how this was going to turn out.

"Where are you from?" I asked detecting an accent.

"Nova Scotia, me lad," he replied and proceeded to launch into a loud rendition of a maritime ditty at the top of his lungs, annoying some passengers and amusing others. Several others joined in the merriment singing along to the Newfie tune, "I'se the b'y dat builds the boats. And I'se da by dat sails 'em." We rocked our way to New Westminster with our own on board folkie. When we arrived at our final destination he staggered out happy and safe quickly disappearing into the night.

Of course there are times when you have to take a stand to make sure the safety of everyone on the bus is honoured. Donna, a fellow driver, says, "When someone starts acting up on my bus, I just go into mad mama mode. It works like a charm. I'll say, 'You boys stop that right now. That's no way to behave on a bus.' And they calm down like bad school kids who've been told off."

It's not just drunks who can test your patience. In my position as an operator I get plenty of opportunity to practice shifting the energy of even the most entrenched grouch.

Looking For Win-Win

"Ding. Ding. Ding. Ding," I looked in the mirror and saw an elderly lady at the back of the bus pulling the chime cord again and again. She appeared to be late and was expressing her frustration at each and every stop, including red traffic lights and crosswalks full of pedestrians. "Please only pull the bell when you want to get out," I called to her.

She ignored me and continued to ring the bell again and again. I finally got on the overhead speaker and announced loud and clear, "I apologize for all the noise on the bus. The chime seems to be stuck on a woman's finger. To tell you the truth, my mother doesn't get out much these days, and it appears she's very eager to catch the shoe sale at the Army & Navy store. This bickering back and forth is a time honoured family tradition, but I do apologize for the theatrical interruptions on your ride."

I took another look in the rear-view mirror and saw a small smile crease her lips. She quickly turned to look out the window as if amused by her own reaction to my announcement. A few blocks later she got up to leave. Everyone in the bus was watching curiously to see how this played out. "This is my stop, driver. I will not ring the bell. Thank you for your sense of humour. Have a good day." Her face split into a big grin as she left. I let out a sigh of relief, realizing that I had averted a possible confrontation by hitting it straight on the head with humour.

Freebies

Most big cities have to deal with the problem of people wanting free rides. When I first began driving in Vancouver, I got about five requests per week for free rides. Twenty years later as I was ready to retire, it had increased to a staggering ten to twenty per eight-hour shift. To me, this indicates a real social struggle. When I was young I would have been mortified to not pay my own way, but nowadays many people, and not just those who are down and out, feel that they are entitled to free public transit. The company, naturally, wants to collect fares from everyone. At the same time they don't want their employees to be at risk. Tricky!

From my perspective in the driver's seat, I also feel it's important that all passengers are treated with respect and dignity. In the case of the free riders I believe it's important to show compassion. Sometimes I, too, struggle to not feel irritated or superior to those who want a free ride. When it comes right down to it, if there was no one to pick up on the street, I would not have a job. I keep my cool by reminding myself that I am happy passengers keep showing up for me to ferry them to their destination.

White Knight Moves

"Are you alright?" I said quietly to a woman that looked tense and nervous as she boarded the bus. She waited for the man behind her to pay and walk to the back of the bus.

"No" she whispered, "that man had been following me. He kept looking at me while I was waiting for the bus. I am feeling scared."

"Okay. I have an idea. Go find yourself a seat and in a few blocks ring the bell. Leave by the back door and immediately walk up to the front door and get back in. Do you understand?"

She nodded in agreement even though she looked a bit confused. A few stops later, the bell rang and she exited the back doors. Sure enough, the man jumped up and followed her off the bus. She hurried to the front doors and hopped in before he knew what was happening. I closed the door and drove away.

"Well done," I said observing the look of relief in her face, "Good to see you again so soon."

"Oh thank you so much, I didn't know what to do. He was really creeping me out. Thanks for getting rid of him. I appreciate that."

"The bus is a safe place and most drivers will help you out if you just let them know what is going on. Have a safe and happy night."

She walked a little taller and lighter to a seat near the back.

A Tommy T Quip

The $20 Bus Fare

A well-dressed man squints at the fare box trying to figure out how much to pay.

"When was the last time you took a bus?" I ask.

"It's probably been 15 or 20 years," he responds.

"Excellent," I reply, "That'll be $20 please."

To his look of shock, I quickly add, "Hey, a dollar a year is a fair price to keep the buses on the road all this time until your car broke down."

We both laugh.
"Next time, get yourself a Toyota like mine. It's older than I am and runs better."

Chapter 12
The Art of Acknowledgement at Work

"What you leave behind is not what is engraved in stone monuments, but what is woven into the lives of others."
~Pericles

I love the scene in the film *Crocodile Dundee* where he walks down the streets of Manhattan, his first time in a big city, and says politely to every individual in the throngs of people, "G'day. G'day. G'day." He doesn't know - but we do - that it's impossible to have a relationship with everyone in a city of millions. His attempt to do so is hilarious, although admirable.

For me, the Art of Acknowledgement is my way of doing just that: creating relationships in a world that seems bent on eliminating them. But, don't take my word for it, use the Art of Acknowledgment and see the results for yourself. You will be pleasantly surprised at the positive responses that will flow back your way. There is magic in the air, and it is coming for you if only you have your butterfly net of awareness handy and open at all times.

When you get the impulse to say something friendly, kind and complimentary...act immediately. Hurry! You only have five seconds, but remember to deliver your words of acknowledgement from the heart with courage and courtesy.

The 7 Steps to the Art of Acknowledgement:

1. Be aware of other people - they ache to be seen
2. Notice something nice or unique about them
3. Tell them cleanly what it was that you noticed
4. Use sweet words in all that you say
5. Have no expectations about how your words are received
6. Be playful, but respectful

7. Smile inwardly and silently acknowledge yourself for having made a positive difference in sending another ripple of kindness out into the world

Communicating with others is now second nature to me, but then again I'm naturally outgoing. If you are shy or self-conscious, it may push your edges to casually chat with strangers. Below are some practical tips on how to get started. This may push your comfort, but trust me it's a good stretch.

Start Out Small

Acknowledge one person you meet today. It could be a clerk in a store, a bank teller, a street cleaner or the person who serves you coffee in a restaurant. These people are particularly open to receiving a few sweet words as their job is to be of service and they rarely receive personal feedback or compliments.

At Home

When was the last time you told your partner how good they look as they head off to work? Love has many forms, but the simplest way to say we love someone is to say something nice to them.

Children glow when given a compliment - especially if it's put into perspective. "I'm so proud that you stood up for your friend when the school bully was being mean to him." It's easy to remember with small kids, but teens yearn for approval as well. A friend recalls her daughter accusing her one day with, "Could you walk in the door and say 'Hi, how was your day?' before you let me know all the things I haven't done yet?" With family, it's way too easy to forget to let them know that they are important to you and that you appreciate them.

Improving your communication with your loved ones lays the foundation for taking the Art of Acknowledgement outdoors. It's a fact that you are a product of your environment, so using the Art of Acknowledgement with your family gives your children a template for how to be kind and thoughtful with others.

Use People's Names

The next time you go to a restaurant ask your waiter their name and then introduce yourself and anyone else in your party. When you need something, say, "Gloria, could I get another glass of water, please?" or whatever it is that you require. Simply by using their name, you acknowledge them and keep the humanness in the conversation. Not only does it make everyone feel better, you will almost invariably get better service.

Try this next time you have to deal with customer support on the phone. Often they tell you their name when the conversation is initiated. Remember it. Write it down if you have to. When you run into a obstacle, ask for help directly, "David, I'm so glad to talk to you. I really need some help." You will be amazed at how much better service and problem solving happens when you speak to them as though you now know them. Always end the conversation by thanking them personally, "Thanks David. Have a good day," or my personal favourite, "Thanks Susan, you deserve the Angel of the Day award. I really appreciate your help." They are going to get off the phone feeling good about themselves and the job they do. What better gift could you give to another human being than to let them know that they have done something to make the world a bit better today?

Compliment Public Workers
You ever seen the folks that walk around with long-handled pinchers picking up garbage on the street? Thank them, "Thanks for making the city a nicer place." Or simply say, "Great work. Thanks." and give them a thumbs up signal and a smile.

Humour works well:
"Hope you clean up this mess before you go home," is a fun way to catch a flag girl's attention as you slowly move through a construction zone. They have a thankless job and I love to lighten their day.

I had to pass such a crew repeatedly as I went back and forth on my route. On one trip I thumbed my nose at a flag girl as I waited, yet again, for the signal to pass the worksite. She responded to my playfulness by thumbing her nose back at me. One trip we had a long wait while a backhoe moved into position. I got on the speaker system and asked the passengers on one side of the bus to thumb their noses at her as the bus slowly passed by her. Looking back in the rear view mirror, I could see her laughing hysterically. It certainly added fun and play to her day and for all the passengers who enjoyed playing along.

Acknowledge Families
Being a mom may be the least acknowledged job on the planet. Traipsing around with small kids and strollers is not easy. You make a mother's day when you notice how

cute, beautiful, happy and polite her children are and you tell her so. "I see you have your mother very well trained", I direct this to the child in the stroller, "I hope your remember to tip her well." Upon leaving I once again speak to the baby, "Bye now, come again, and bring your Mom."

Sometimes when I see a family out, I'll throw the compliment to the father, "Hey Dad, beautiful family, have fun out there."

Friendlier Queues

This is the ideal place to start up a conversation by making a friendly, complimentary comment to your neighbour in a line up. It passes the time and makes everyone feel happier and more positive.

Be Kind to Street People

Pity doesn't sustain people, but genuine kindness can. It's not easy living on the street, and I imagine it's not much fun depending on others for spare change to make your way through life. Even if you don't agree with giving money to street beggars, acknowledging their existence with a smile. Saying, "Have a good day," doesn't take a lot of effort and makes them feel like human beings who deserve the same respect as anyone. On occasion, I've even invited a street kid into a Starbucks for a coffee and a bit of warmth.

Remember that respect is the backbone of any exchange, but of course adding fun and humour gets the message across even better. Like any 'Art', the Art of Acknowledgement gets better with practice. Over time as you see the impact of your words on others, you too will soon become comfortable chatting and playing with strangers. By being friendly, you make the world a friendlier place.

Making Changes in Your Work Place:

If you are not sure how you can make a difference in your daily working life, then ask yourself the following questions:

What do you see missing?

Seek the need and fill it. What simple thing could you do (complaining doesn't count as affirmative action) to remedy the situation? Don't go big. Don't decide to take on the CEO of the company. Try something closer to where you work. Some women enjoy bringing home-baked cookies to the office. Do they think that people are hungry? No, they want to bring a homeyness to the workplace and make it a friendlier, nicer environment by connecting to others.

Who needs a bit of tender care?

It's fun to sit with your buddies at lunch break, but who is that person who never seems to be included? Invite them along. Stretch your heart to include others. You may be surprised by who you discover when you talk to them.

What are you passionate about?

Maybe you are an organizer—very advantageous in a messy workplace. Is there a way you can include that passion into your working life? Do you have an eye for photography? Offer to take photos of company events and put them on the company website or in the yearly calendar.

My bus company alone has three thousand drivers, each of whom has the option of being an Ambassador for Change. Multiply that by the number of drivers across the world and you touch almost everyone on the planet. So when people wonder if it makes a difference what you do, I respond enthusiastically with "Yes!" More important: it's not only what you do, it's how you do it. I truly believe that we all want to give even if we don't realize it consciously—giving joy or gifts or service to others just feels good and 'nothing' is more important than that we feel good inside.

From this foundation and root of sweet joy within, we are able to find all the strength we need to get to the next thing in our life. For those of us that understand this and practice it consciously with an 'open heart', life is indeed richer than we previously thought possible. Chase your passion rather than your pension. Benefits of the Art of Acknowledgement in the Workplace:

- Happier staff
- Improved morale
- Declining assault rate
- Modelling to others
- Financial gain: less employee absences and sick leave
- Fewer compensation claims
- Retain staff
- Improve your organization's reputation

A Tommy T Quip

Take A Load Off

"If the food's too heavy, you're welcome to leave it with me, " I say to passengers struggling onto the bus loaded down with bags of groceries.

When they protest, I get inventive, "Hey! I'm just trying to feed a wife and six kids. Any contribution is happily accepted."

To another woman with her week's worth of shopping, "You need something with wheels on it for that load. Or a manservant. The thing with the wheels is much cheaper and a whole lot less hassle."

Chapter 13
Ambassadors for Change

*"Never doubt that a small group of thoughtful,
committed citizens can change the world.
Indeed, it is the only thing
that ever has." ~ Margaret Mead*

T
he Magic of Caring

As bus drivers we bring lovers together, and we tear them apart. We reunite old friends, we join families on holidays or take nervous people to that all important new job interview. We watch community enthusiasms erupt when the local sports team wins. We ferry people to their doctor's appointments or bring them home from the hospital. We act as tour guides for visitors to the city. We help the lost and act as a safe haven for those feeling uncomfortable in a rough part of town. Our uniforms make us stand out and signify that we are trustworthy and approachable.

Part of a Team

As a bus driver I'm out there by myself, and yet I am part of a team. With thousands of drivers we rarely see more than one or two other members of that team unless we are in the depot. Often we pick up our shift on the road and so the only other company person we meet is the driver we relieve or the one that takes over at the end of our day. Much of the time we are autonomous, and yet there is that camaraderie we feel as we wave to each other in passing. I have enjoyed being part of the community of drivers.

While it's as natural as breathing for me to hand out compliments and acknowledgements, there are many people that bring a little extra joy and fun into their workday along with their lunch pail. There are many amazing, happy and helpful bus drivers. Here are just a few who have made a mark by bringing something unique onto their buses and into the lives of their passengers:

Yves is known as The Singing Bus Driver. For years he's entertained passengers as he drives the streets of Ottawa with renditions of popular songs, which he croons a cappella. Was he aiming to be the next candidate for America's Got Talent? No. He simply brought his love of music to work and thousands of riders loved the 'extra' he injected into their day.

A North Vancouver bus driver dresses like Elvis Presley and takes requests for Elvis tunes, thanking his passengers as they leave the bus with an Elvis-style, "Thank-you. Thank-you. Thank-you, very much."

There's John, the Trivia Guy, who keeps everyone's brain cells firing with trivia questions. The first person to guess the correct answer is rewarded with a chocolate bar. He has personally paid for and gifted over 5000 chocolate bars. How sweet is that!

Kirk loves Christmas so much so that he shows up a full hour before his shift in the month before Christmas. Why? To decorate his bus with gift wrapped boxes, lights and a small portable music system powered by his own battery, fake snow and decorations draped throughout the bus he will be driving that day. He dons an authentic Santa beard and red suit that competes with his own rosy cheeks and sparkling eyes, as he "Ho, Ho, Ho's," his way across town brightening the lives of hundreds of people during the holiday season.

Tony loves being a bit of a tour guide, sharing the city's attractions and current events with his passengers by acting as an unofficial but much appreciated promoter of his city. Coming over the Granville Bridge, he calls out over the microphone,

"Just wanted to point out that this 360 degree view is full of all the reasons we live here. What a beautiful city, how blessed we are. What a great day. We knew those dark rain clouds would move away to reveal the snow-capped mountains. It's just like living in your favourite calendar photo.

Keep in mind that we are the envy of everyone who lives anywhere else in Canada. On the right as we come off the bridge, you'll see a beautiful mural, a West Coast scene with whales. A man named Wyland from Hawaii created this mural in 1986 just in time for the World's fair. He returned prior to the 2010 Olympics with a team of painters and completely refurbished the weather beaten wall. He's painted over three hundred large wall murals like this all across the planet. Check out his stunning gallery the next time you are in Lahaina, Maui. It is inspirational. I apologize but you will have to catch another bus to get there."

Hallowe'en is another great opportunity for lots of drivers to let loose and share their exuberance and individuality by joining into the play. Masks, of course, are avoided for safety reasons, yet drivers get very creative in their enthusiasm to bring a bit of joy. Pirates, goblins, draculas and drag queens take over operating the bus system for a colourful night. It's a great way to get involved, adding fun to the community while keeping people safe and out of their cars during a night of partying.

Nalini's smile lights up the front of her bus like sunshine. As you enter you can't miss the fact that the fare box has been transformed into a colourful and fragrant flowerbed to welcome her passengers.

Cecile may be short, but she makes up for it with style by wearing an artificial Plumeria (it's a flower) in her hair that faces the passengers as they board. "They climb the stairs and immediately smile when they see my flower. If I happen to not wear it, they always look so disappointed. It's so simple, but it creates a bond, especially with my regulars."

Michelle flaunts her vibrant personality by wearing a signature pink scarf as she laughs and chats with her passengers. Full of jokes and personal interaction, she sparkles her way through every working day.

In addition to the individuals who bring fun and engagement to their passengers, I am profoundly grateful to work for a company that allows us to pull our buses over to the curb for two minutes of silence in honour of those who fought in the wars on November 11th, Remembrance Day.

The company supports other ways of connecting to the larger community with electronic signs on the outside of the bus that can be programmed to read: Happy Holidays. Season's Greetings. The signs can also be programmed to support all our local sports teams in hockey, football and soccer with 'Go Canucks Go', 'Go Lions Go', or 'Go Whitecaps Go'. It is a nice touch for building community.

I think one of the most touching stories was what Bill did:
"Give me your coffee cups," Bill would ask his fellow drivers as they stood around the terminus between shifts. "Hurry I have to stick them in my front wheel."

Bill donated his spare time volunteering at a youth camp for challenged kids. One girl at the camp particularly caught his attention and they spent hours together. Bill knew that the chances of her living beyond the age of 16 were remote. Nadine lived on the sixth floor of an apartment on Broadway, Bill's regular route. She asked her Mom to tie a balloon to the balcony railing so Bill could see which apartment she was in.

Bill responded by sticking six white Styrofoam coffee cups in the front left wheel that spun like spikes on a chariot creating a distinctive marker letting her know that this was his bus. Every Wednesday at noon he drove past her apartment waving from the bus and honking his horn as she eagerly waved back to him. He did this for months until one day... the balloon was gone.

Go Forth

> *I believe that we do as much good by*
> *bringing a heartfelt smile to someone's*
> *face as we can by any act of charity.*
> *- Tommy Transit*

As bus drivers, we are not just ambassadors representing our company or putting our city in the best light. We can also stand proud in the fact that our "average Joe" job provides us with unique opportunities to reach out and make a difference in the lives of the hundreds of thousands of people we each meet every year. If your sphere of influence isn't as great as mine has been, do not be deterred. Trust that every person you touch with kindness will absorb your joy and, in turn, they will be inspired to let it bubble forth in some way you cannot know.

I invite anyone—bus driver or not—to pick up the baton and be an ambassador for change by playing with the tools I have outlined in this book. And I mean play!

The whole idea is to have fun with this, to stretch yourself in your job and your life by realizing that what you do and how you do it has a real impact on others. Just as important: Don't underestimate the powerful impact that acknowledging others has on your own health, happiness, well-being and job satisfaction.

As my lovely Irish friend Teresa chirps in her delightful brogue, "Keep 'er lit, Tommy keep 'er lit." It's good advice and most days I create the intention of keeping my inner light shining so that I am able to stay on purpose.

I offer this book to my fellow drivers, my company, and all those who work with the public. We truly have the opportunity to be bus drivers on a mission.

For me, it's Mission Accomplished.

A Tommy T Quip

Port-a-pottie Repartee

I jumped off the bus for a quick pit stop at a portable toilet on a construction site in the middle of my bus route with 30 passengers on board. Getting back on the bus, one of the passengers called out: "Did you wash your hands?"

"No," I said, "That's why I wear these gloves." As I slip them on I add, "But it makes it difficult to get the zipper down."

A woman pipes up, "I bet it's harder to get it up."

Dead silence on the bus! My mind reels and I quickly quip, "We're still talking about the zipper, right?"

The bus explodes with laughter.

Epilogue
A Bus Man's Holiday

"There are really only three types of people: Those who make things happen, those who watch things happen, and those who say, "What happened?" ~ Author Unknown

"**H**e's the one! He's the one!" The woman behind the bar puts her hands on her hips and nodding in my direction declares, "I want you to drive my bus next summer."

"What bus?" I inquire.

"You walked right past it, are you blind?"

"That old thing," I retort, "Holy Moly, I thought it was part of the flower bed."

"That old bus runs better than you do." she snaps back. This lady definitely has an edge.

I had been dog sitting for a friend on Galiano Island, one of the Southern Gulf Islands in the Straight of Georgia. I was thrilled, but the dog was not. She sulked for two days. On the third night, I ladled a large dollop of gravy onto her food, which turned the tables. Now we were friends.

I had jumped at my friend's offer of a quiet retreat to begin writing down the ideas for a book that had been percolating in my head for some time. No one knew I was here and my phone didn't work in "heaven." The words flowed and the pages filled, in between regular dog walks along the shore in the fresh ocean breeze. I was in the local island pub for just a few minutes so Michele could access the ATM machine to get some money I loaned her. I fell into conversation with the pub owner. "Wow, nice place. I love it," I said surveying the sprawling wooden pub with a large deck overlooking a green lawn.

In the middle of our chat, Michele returned and seeing me engaged in conversation with an attractive woman, slapped two twenties on my chest and said with a big smirk, "Thanks for last night, it was fun." Then spinning on her heels, she left me red faced with the pub owner laughing so hard she almost swallowed her cigarette. After regaining her composure she said, "Forty dollars! Wow, very nice."

"Hey you didn't see the $100 coupon she had with this cash. I'm not cheap you know."

"Right! So funny man, what's your name."

"Tommy Transit"

Again she doubled over in laughter and a woman sitting on a barstool joined her. "What kind of dumb name is that?"

This was all too much for me. Acting miffed, I took a big slug of beer and walked out of the bar, her words following me as the door slammed.

"So are you stiffing me for a beer, Mr. Transit?"

Several minutes later I returned tossing a page from the Vancouver Province newspaper on the counter. "Here's my business card." The full-page article had been written a year earlier and had a photo of me behind the wheel of a Vancouver city bus. The write-up was in the good news section about people that had made an impact in the community.

"Holy Cow," she said, "He really is Tommy Transit!"

The next thing I knew, I was taking a test run in the beaten up red jalopy she called a bus along the winding roads of Galiano Island to the pristine Montague Harbour, with bobbing boats in the marina and beautiful adjacent camp grounds. I now had a vision of how my bus man's holiday would unfold.

Escorting a pub bus filled with happy drinkers safely back to their boats or tents is a very different undertaking than driving transit in a city of millions. It's a perfect stage for the "entertainer" in me to come out and thrive. Like a crazy bus in a third world country, the steering wheel is surrounded by musical instruments: a tambourine, cow bell and cymbals with which I add percussive hits to the music blasting from the speakers. The passengers sing along laughing at my antics.

As we slide down the hill to the valley, I make this announcement, "Ladies and Gentlemen, please take a moment to enjoy the sights of our fair isle of Galiano. On the right, we have a field of Martian Poodles." All heads turn. "Oh wait a minute. I am so sorry. Those are freshly shaved llamas and alpacas. Easy to get them confused."

As I check in the rear view mirror, I see that many on the seven-minute trek across the island come to Galiano year after year. It's a twenty-seven year old legend and I am just a recent participant, but I relish the opportunity of interacting, being goofy and playing with people from all over the globe.

I shout above the rattling bus, "Very few of you may realize that the Hummingbird Pub has undergone a change of status. It is a first class establishment now with new rules of conduct. Upon application to the Restaurant Association of BC last winter, we re-wallpapered the bathrooms, we ordered new napkins and reprinted the menu. Because of these changes, most of you are in trouble and will probably not get past the bouncer. I don't know what to say, they have redone the dress code." At this point I whip off my driver's hat and put on a two-foot high black Guinness top hat. "Remember, fine dining demands fine threads," I add as the bus pulls into the pub parking lot and everyone tumbles out laughing.

My life continues to be magical and rich with possibilities, filled with daily miraculous adventures that I am able to share with my family and friends. I invite everyone to track me down wherever I am on the globe.

"Remember, you are awesome. Have a fabulous day, because you deserve no less."

The bus door closes with a hiss.

Places to Visit

To stay in touch with Tom and follow his antics:
www.TommyTransit.com

Michele Hall, What Works Media:
www.WhatWorksMedia.ca

Coast Mountain Bus Company:
www.CoastMountainBus.com

Denis Waitley: www.Waitley.com

Esther Hicks - Abraham's Teachings: www.Abraham-Hicks.com

Institute of Hearth Math: www.HeartMath.org

Mary Manin Morissey: www.MaryMorrissey.com

Jeffrey Armstrong: www.JeffreyArmstrong.com

Mel Robbins: www.MelRobbins.com

Mary Robinson Reynolds: She has created The Acknowledgement Movie, The Make A Difference Movie and many more: www.MakeADifference.com

The Validation Movie has had over 6.5 million views:
http://www.youtube.com/watch?v=Cbk980jV7Ao

Brock Tully's Kindness Foundation:
www.KindnessFoundation.com